WOMEN
AND EMPOWERMENT

WOMEN AND EMPOWERMENT
Strategies for Increasing Autonomy

C. Margaret Hall

Department of Sociology
Georgetown University
Washington, D.C.

● HEMISPHERE PUBLISHING CORPORATION
A member of the Taylor & Francis Group
Washington   Philadelphia   London

WOMEN AND EMPOWERMENT: Strategies for Increasing Autonomy

1 2 3 4 5 6 7 8 9 0   E B E B   9 8 7 6 5 4 3 2

This book was set in Times Roman by Hemisphere Publishing Corporation. The editor was Heather Jefferson; the cover designer was Kathleen Ernst; the production supervisor was Peggy M. Rote; and the typesetters were Darrell D. Larsen, Jr., Pamela R. Quayle, and Laurie Strickland.
Printing and binding by Edwards Brothers, Inc.

A CIP catalog record for this book is available from the British Library.

∞ The paper in this publication meets the requirements of the ANSI Standard Z39.48-1984(Permanence of Paper)

Library of Congress Cataloging in Publication Data

Hall, C. Margaret (Constance Margaret)
    Women and empowerment: strategies for increasing autonomy / C. Margaret Hall.
        p.   cm.
    Includes bibliographical references and index.

    1. Women's rights. 2. Feminism. 3. Autonomy (Psychology)
    I. Title.
HQ1236.H27   1992
305.42—dc20   91-37977
ISBN 1-56032-266-7 (case)   CIP
ISBN 1-56032-267-5 (paper)

To my daughters,
Elizabeth, Tanya, and J'Amy

Contents

Preface

Women and Empowerment: Strategies for Increasing Autonomy is a synthesis of others' research and an application of a new clinical sociological theory—identity empowerment theory—to current patterns in women's behavior. My assumptions in interpreting existing data are that women want to improve their effectiveness in their own lives, and that they want to be in strong positions to live fully in both individual and social contexts.

Women and Empowerment shows how women's decisions direct their lives into private or public spheres of activity. Life-history data illustrate some of the nuances in the interplay between women's personal activities and their contributions to society and history. Women's abilities to say yes or no to their significant others, and to formulate meaningful long-range goals for their own pursuits and achievements, are determining factors in their fulfillment.

The overall attempt in assembling these data and research findings is to advance human rights in the direction of gaining respect, honor, and happiness for all. Although most of the ideas suggested evolve from women's experiences in the United States, some attention is paid to assessing conditions of women throughout the world, as well as international feminism.

In the final analysis, what women do with their lives remains an individual decision. We cannot risk waiting for equality to come to us through adequate legislation. We must claim our own equality in order to live fully now.

Women and Empowerment encourages individual and social assertions of women's rights and responsibilities, and urges women to assist each other in accomplishing these quests. It is not so much that women want to seize power from men, but rather that they want their fair share, and they want to live cooperatively rather than competitively.

Women and Empowerment suggests that the essential choice women must make is between values, and that integrity is the heart of all grassroots activism. Everyday living is a real arena for political action, and women already have much expertise on how to use wisdom to survive.

Although most of the suggestions implied by *Women and Empowerment* apply to men as well as to women, it will be women rather than men who follow through by changing their behavior. The reason for women's openness to change is not so much that they know better than men that these are life-giving principles, but rather that women are hurting more than men in their current circumstances; they are more desperate to make changes to relieve or transform their pressured and restricted lives. An exception to this pattern of receptivity to *Women and Empowerment* is men who may be described as "wounded warriors." When men learn that the machismo principle is destructive to themselves and to others, they willingly turn to new ideas to empower them through putting their lives together in meaningful and effective ways.

My effort to address the interests of women in different social classes and varied ethnic groups is more limited than I want it to be. I have generalized more than I have made specific studies of the wide variety of women's experiences in *Women and Empowerment*. In the final analysis, however, I believe women have more in common with each other than the diversity in their experiences suggests. Furthermore, whatever the social class, ethnic group, or cultural and historical context, all women are beholden to the male authority structures of mainstream society. If generalizations made in *Women and Empowerment* do not accurately represent gender relations within specific social classes or ethnic groups, discussions and interpretations should be applied to male dominance in the upper classes of society.

Women and Empowerment is intended to rally women to make decisions about their personal and public lives. We live in times of great resistance to change alongside great change. We cannot afford to be complacent about the world as we find it. My hope is that readers will pioneer in creating new forms and processes in relationships, as well as innovative social goals.

C. Margaret Hall

Acknowledgments

I am personally and professionally indebted to many people for the ideas and facts presented here. I know that *Women and Empowerment* would not come alive without the life-history data, so I first thank the women I interviewed in clinical and research settings. I also thank the clinical sociologists who guided me most in the analyses of life-history data and other research: Janet Mancini Billson, Estelle Disch, Elizabeth Clark, and Melvyn Fein.

Sociologist and anthropologist colleagues who helped me to integrate the theoretical base of *Women and Empowerment* are Timothy Wickham-Crowley, Robert Bell, and Gwendolyn Mikell. As always, my colleagues in women's studies at Georgetown University are supportive and questioning in their assessments of my work, particularly Leona Fisher.

Women in the local community contributed to the formulation of my ideas. My participation in monthly discussion groups enabled me to make the all-important bridge between sociological practice and actual living.

The research assistance of Lisa Gabbert, Suzanne Baker, and Lisa McDonald was invaluable. I am particularly grateful to Suzanne Baker for her

long-range interests and enthusiasm. Without her close scrutiny of library resources, this book would not have seen the light of day.

Advisers at Taylor & Francis/Hemisphere gave their continuing interest
and support: Ron Wilder, Carolyn Baker, and Bill Begell. With their encouragement, *Women and Empowerment* took its present form.

Members of my own family inspired me and gave their support tirelessly
and patiently during times of concentrated effort: my husband, Robert Cole; my
daughters, Elizabeth, Tanya, and J'Amy Cole; my mother, Madeline Hall; and
my mother-in-law, Bella Cole. Their different challenges helped me to understand.

C. Margaret Hall

Chapter 1

Introduction

Women and Empowerment: Strategies for Increasing Automony is a study of women's deepest desires to live productively and cooperatively. Women's experiences are examined and distilled in order to portray how women make changes that will increase their effectiveness in personal and public domains, as well as changes that will increase the scope of their actions.

Women and Empowerment analyzes women's behavior and concerns by applying a specific clinical sociological theory—identity empowerment theory (Hall, 1990b)—to life history data. The 10 concepts of identity empowerment theory derive from both classical sociological theory (Caute, 1967; Cooley, 1962, 1964; Durkheim, 1965, 1966, 1984; Gerth & Mills, 1946; Mead, 1967; Weber, 1977) and contemporary sociological theory (Becker, 1950; Berger & Luckmann, 1966; Blau, 1967; Blumer, 1969; Goffman, 1973; Rosenberg, 1979; Shibutani, 1955; Smelser, 1962). Identity empowerment theory is also strongly influenced by the relatively new subdisciplines of clinical sociology and sociological practice (Clark, 1990; Fritz, 1985; Glass, 1979; Glass & Fritz, 1982; Glassner & Freedman, 1979; Lee, 1979; Moreno & Glassner, 1979; Wirth, 1931).

Women and Empowerment suggests modes of explanation by examining the impact of trends in families, religion, and work on different groups of women and on individual women. In reaching her conclusions, the author has drawn upon more than 20 years of experience as a clinical sociologist and research interviewer in making her interpretations.

Five hundred subjects were interviewed to collect life history data for this study on women's empowerment. Of those 500 interviews, 400 were conducted in a clinical setting and 100 were conducted in a research setting. Because crisis intervention was the original impetus for the collection of four fifths of the life histories, special attention is given in these analyses to how effective and expeditious change can be accomplished in individual women's lives.

Distillations of the life history data are used to illustrate how families, religion, work, world conditions for women, and ideologies of feminism have significant consequences for women's thoughts, feelings, decisions, and actions. In assessing these influences, the author considers social class, ethnic group, and age as having a critical impact on women's behavior.

Time frames in *Women and Empowerment* span from women's hourly and daily behavior, to historical views of women (Beard, 1971) and evolutionary perspectives (Alland, 1967). The formal clinical research and interviews for this study were conducted by the author in the United States; however, some comparisons of findings from the life histories are made with other social scientists' analyses of women's experiences in contrasting cultural and social settings.

SOCIAL SOURCES OF MOTIVATION AND ACTION

General sociological and clinical sociological theories focus simultaneously on individuals, especially as members of specific groups, and on the social sources of an individual's being, motivation, and action. In contrast to intrapsychic explanations of personal and public behavior (Freud, 1982), in evaluating influences on individual and group behavior, sociologists account for as comprehensive a social context as possible (Berteaux, 1981).

The premise of identity empowerment theory is that women's behavior and quality of life can be changed by increasing their awareness of the strength of social influences and of the interplay between intended and unintended consequences of women's decisions and actions. Although the relative separateness of women's varied ethnic groups and social classes differentially limits their opportunities (Bernard, 1981), identity empowerment theory postulates that all women can make some constructive changes to enhance and improve their situations, however restricted those situations.

To facilitate the accomplishment of creative changes in women's lives, identity empowerment theory is used to suggest ways out of the morass of stresses and controls that dominate women. However, the issue of recognition of women's choices is crucial, because if the restrictions on women are not recognized and dealt with by women themselves, those restrictions will necessarily have deadening—and deadly—consequences for all women.

By consciously connecting personal and public aspects of their lives, women can enlarge their worlds and participate in broader spheres of activity traditionally reserved exclusively for men (Bernard, 1981). This impact is especially evident in the world of work. However, family and religion are also critical dimensions to consider in assessing the personal and public aspects of women's lives. Women's empowerment is the deliberate integration of women's biographies with society's history, a feat that can transform women's individual and social realities (Mills, 1967).

IDENTITY EMPOWERMENT THEORY

There are 10 concepts of identity empowerment theory: self, dyad, triad, family, religion, definition of the situation, reference group, class, culture, and society (see Appendix I for definitions of these concepts). Women's realization of these 10 selected subjective and objective dimensions of individual and group experience neutralize some of the inhibitions and entrapments endemic to the conditions of their gender, age, and social class.

Women's awareness that they play an active role in history may loosen some of the restrictions they experience from their domestic role expectations (Beard, 1971). Identifying women's real interests, and deliberately sharing those interests with other women, increases women's individual and social motivations to work to change present circumstances (Caute, 1967; Mills, 1967). Although women are an extremely heterogeneous group, a few experiences—for example, family and work—are common denominators and can orient them toward meeting some of their diverse needs.

Just as innovative conceptualizations in the social sciences lead to new syntheses of established knowledge and create new knowledge (Kuhn, 1970), the recently emerging discipline of women's studies presents new paradigms and new views of individual and social realities (Andersen, 1988). It is in such a spirit of exploration and innovation that readers are invited to consider some of the new views of woman, women, and society that are explicit and implicit in identity empowerment theory and *Women and Empowerment*.

SUBSTANTIVE CONCERNS

Unless specific substantive applications are made from sociological theories, the theories may seem too abstract and too far removed from reality. *Women and Empowerment* uses both microsociological and macrosociological dimensions of women's experiences to illustrate restrictions on women and how women's actions are freed.

At the most microsociological level of analysis, the centrality and realities of the self are examined. Because women of all ages, classes, and ethnic groups are thoroughly conditioned and habituated to place others before themselves in thinking and acting, it is vital that women give highest priority to deepening their understanding of who they are and what they really want to do with their lives.

Gender is inextricably related to self-concept. Stereotypes and the expectations of women associated with those stereotypes permeate each woman's reality, especially during the earliest developmental stages of socialization. Only by recognizing and understanding the strength of these pervasive influences can women develop self sufficiently to be relatively independent of those influences.

Families are the most significant emotional contexts of women's and men's lives. Women, dramatically more so than men, are bound by family responsibilities. Consequently, family ties need to be scrutinized and assessed before other avenues of activity are explored. Self and gender, in large part, derive from the emotional programming people receive from their families. It is essential that women acknowledge the complex interrelationships of these factors in order to effectively carve out more freedom for themselves.

Religion is another traditional site of women's oppression. Religion can be an insidiously powerful influence on women's lives, because it creates and exerts inner controls on their behavior. Although religion may be a source of expansive motivation for some women, generally speaking religion tends to have the effect of limiting or inhibiting women's lives, whatever their age, ethnic group, or social class. It is not so much the overall substance of particular denominational or sectarian beliefs that has such restrictive effects, but rather the emphasis within specific religious belief systems that is placed on women's family responsibilities and women's duty to be obedient. Major world religions, with the possible exception of Taoism, project many negative connotations of women and women's values. Women's freedom and empowerment reside in women facing the enormous strength of religious influences in their lives—whether or not individual women are religious themselves—and in women's persistence in growing and pursuing long-range goals of their own, in spite of the restrictions on them.

Women's everyday work, both in and out of the home, is influential in defining their life chances. Receiving financial and emotional rewards for work is essential for women's well-beings in their personal and public worlds. In most family situations, however, the combination of family and work demands overburdens middle- and lower-class women with stress. The stress results from women being held responsible for children and for family and household chores, in addition to work assignments out of the home.

The circumstances of women's lives throughout the world affect all women. Women can learn a great deal about themselves and their options by learning about the contrasting conditions of women in diverse historical and cultural settings. Although there are many repeated patterns in women's varied cultural and historical circumstances, each situation is necessarily unique. Through examining a broad range of women's historical and cultural experiences, women can identify themselves and their own interests more clearly. This identification strengthens their sense of relatedness to other women as a distinct gender class as well as their sense of relatedness to humankind as a whole.

Feminism is a political ideology that expressly addresses women's experiences of subordination to men and women's need for equity. Although some women may not agree with or understand the tenets of feminism, it is important that all women take a stand in relation to feminism. This ideology is not a value and belief system that women can afford to ignore. Historically, feminism has influenced legislation and social attitudes, and today women in the United States stand on the shoulders of women activists who have gone before them. Women need to deepen their knowledge of feminism and act with that knowledge.

Women's individual and collective empowerment results from their awareness and actions in relation to self, gender, family, religion, work, world conditions of women, and the ideology of feminism. Women's individual empowerment, as well as their collective empowerment, are forces for social change in that broad social patterns result from women's individual decisions and actions. When women's perceptions, priorities, and behavior change, the world outside must adapt to them. Although legislative changes are essential and necessary to promote equity throughout a society, women's values and attitudes must also protect women and serve their real interests at all times.

DIRECTION

Women's empowerment can be thought of as a direction that beckons each and every woman. It is the invitation to live fully and to become the person each woman wants to be.

Even when all contingencies of gender equality are legislated effectively, women's integrity, decisions, and actions will continue to be of paramount importance in defining every situation of their lives. Women's empowerment goes far beyond obtaining a legal minimum of coerced equality, to achieving increased self-respect and life-satisfaction and showing concern for the well-being of all human beings.

Given the fact that the United States does not yet have legalized equality between women and men, the direction of women's empowerment in the United States necessarily includes reaching that particular legislative goal through women's political activity. In the most essential respect, however, women's empowerment is a means to achieve many different kinds of changes that will enhance the quality of life for all.

The selected substantive concerns outlined above are described more fully in *Women and Empowerment*. Each of these areas of investigation provides clues to solving the puzzle of women's empowerment and implies stages in women's journey of empowerment.

Studying the empowerment process shows women how to understand more fully the vital signs of their weaknesses and strengths in their everyday lives. In this context, *Women and Empowerment* is a handbook or guide for both women's survival and their fulfillment.

CHOICES

In order to move in the direction of empowerment, women must make specific choices. Although options may be dazzlingly varied, given the rich contrasts in the particular circumstances of women, the following list suggests some of the concerns that women need to take seriously if they are to live as fully as possible.

1 Women must consciously and deliberately choose to live fully if their other choices—about family, religion, and work—are to be effective.

2 Women must choose to see their lives in the broadest possible social context if they wish to expand their vision and increase their options.

3 Women must choose to become aware of the subtleties and intricacies in the relationships between their private and public domains if they are to function optimally.

4 Women must choose to see the interdependence of their individual status and the status of other women throughout the world if they are to understand themselves fully.

5 Women must choose where they stand in relation to feminism if they are to know the depth of the influence of gender in their lives.

6 Women must choose to end their oppression themselves, rather than wait for legislation or other people to accomplish this for them, if they are to be truly empowered.

GENERALIZATIONS

At the outset, a few generalizations can be made about women's empowerment. Although there are necessarily numerous exceptions to any generalizations about individual experience and social trends, a picture of some tendencies can be gained by considering these patterns.

1 Hypothetically, women's empowerment is in the interest of all women and all men, even though women and men may not realize this.

2 As each effort toward empowerment meets with resistance, courage and persistence are essential to make empowering changes.

3 Although different social classes and ethnic groups show marked contrasts in the quality of the experiences of women members of those groups, all women are ultimately interested in surviving social pressures and in living the kinds of lives they really want to live.

4 The experiences of women worldwide are significant influences on the limits and freedoms of women in the United States.

5 Only women can achieve their own empowerment, although men may be willing to make some legislative changes to achieve degrees of equity between women and men.

6 Feminism is a useful means of organizing the interests and political goals of women.

PROPOSITIONS

Propositions go further toward explaining women's empowerment than descriptive generalizations. Propositions relate more directly to particular hypotheses of identity empowerment theory and to particular applications of this theory to women's lives. Life history data need to be collected to further substantiate the following tentative propositions.

1 To the extent that women become more empowered, they are able to live a more satisfying life.

2 Family, religion, and work are more significant determinants of the status and quality of life that women enjoy than are other realms of social activity.

3 Women's empowerment has individual and social consequences for everyone in society.

4 Women's status in other countries has an impact on women's status in the United States.

5 Feminism heightens women's awareness of the ways in which gender defines their values and actions.

6 Women's life histories and the history of the society in which women live are connected whether or not women deliberately make this connection themselves. Moreover, the histories of women and their societies influence each other.

Chapter 2

Questions

Before embarking on this study and analysis of women's empowerment, some questions must be asked. A review of research in the field of gender roles suggests nuances about women and families, religion, and work that must be examined. This gender perspective needs to be focused clearly so that the possibilities, probabilities, and prospects for women's empowerment can be understood.

Although the scope of sociology is much broader than most academic disciplines (Gordon, 1988), early sociological treatises and research were gender blind (Kandal, 1988). In making generalizations about human beings, researchers have been tardy or reluctant to recognize that historically, women's lives and experiences have differed qualitatively from those of men (Linton, 1936). Even contemporary research frequently fails to recognize the full contribution of women's work through the ages (Kessler-Harris, 1981).

Since the 1970s, feminist scholarship has documented some of the differences between the sexual controls on women and on men (Dinnerstein, 1976). These social processes are not new, and a historical perspective demonstrates both the persistence of inequalities (Fitzpatrick, 1990) and the part gender plays in all kinds of social inequality (Curtis, 1986; Curtis & MacCorquodale, 1990).

Although radical changes in social values may be dependent on economic and structural conditions (Mannheim, 1936), gender relations can promote some kinds of changes (Tiryakian, 1981). Knowing more about women's varied experiences and the influence of contemporary feminism enables us to have a deeper understanding of the changing everyday negotiations between women and men (Sydie, 1987; Wallace, 1989).

Conceptualizations of human nature must necessarily include a consideration of women's behavior if they are to be effective (Rosenberg & Turner, 1981; Sieber, 1974). When one considers the lifespan as a significant unit of investigation (Berger, 1990), one can see more clearly the influence on individual and social behavior of particular structures, such as language (Cohn, 1989), and of the new values and beliefs of feminism (Malson, Barr, Wihl, & Wyer, 1989).

DO WOMEN AND MEN EXPERIENCE SELF DIFFERENTLY?

At the outset, it must be considered whether women and men understand and experience self differently. Although the substantive circumstances of men's and women's lives differ dramatically, there are some characteristics of self that women and men have in common.

The fact that human beings are distinguished by their capacity to reflect means that women and men alike have that ability. It appears, however, that people who reflect purposefully need to have a certain level of education before they can make realistic and accurate assessments about their situations, or have an adequate amount of leisure time in which to reflect. Those with heavily pressured lives are less able to reflect and examine their lives (Berger, 1990).

When women and men view themselves with some degree of objectivity, they begin to distinguish their own conditioning (Hewitt, 1990). All people are conditioned in different ways, but frequently ethnic, class, and cultural conditioning are acknowledged and examined before gender conditioning. Perhaps this awareness—or lack of awareness—is because gender conditioning is so close to people that they take it for granted; therefore they do not question or even see its influence in their lives.

Women and men alike are either traditional or modern in their orientations to life and in their articulations of self. It is sometimes difficult to distinguish real self from institutional conditioning. In recent years, increasing numbers of both women and men have been more hedonistic, focusing on their impulses as their real selves (Turner, 1976).

In considering the deeper levels of self as sources of motivation for our behavior, the emotional circumstances of our socialization and conditioning must be examined (Franks & McCarthy, 1989). When considering the influence of self both on people's personal lives and on their lives in society at large, however, some of the differences in self between women and men become clear. Because women's activities are generally much more restricted than are men's activities, it can be inferred that women's self is correspondingly limited in its view of choices and the world at large (Zaretsky, 1976).

TO WHAT EXTENT DOES GENDER INFLUENCE BEHAVIOR?

Gender influences both independently initiated behavior and the reactions of others to that behavior (Chafetz, 1990). This interplay between gender influences and behavioral outcomes is pervasive and has been documented within organizations (Kanter, 1977), as well as in society at large (Matthaei, 1982). Although research has been conducted on motivations of behavior and many behavioral motivations have been recognized (Cohn, 1989; Coleman, 1988), gender may be more influential in determining broad social patterns than has yet been acknowledged (Dinnerstein, 1976).

In order to understand how behaviors associated with gender are learned (Estep, Burt, & Milligan, 1977; Hewitt, 1990; Mason & Bumpass, 1975), it must be recognized that socialization continues beyond the family into the workplace and other social contexts (Gutek, 1985; McKinney & Sprecher, 1989). The study of intercultural differences heightens awareness of the significance of the broader context of women's socialization (Foner & Kertzer, 1978; Mason, Czajka & Arber, 1976; Pescatello, 1973; Spiro, 1979). In addition to considering cultural influences in gender socialization, however, the strength of the biological base of women's sexual behavior must also be acknowledged (Sanday, 1981; Sydie, 1987).

Although gender has its own distinctive patterns and structures (Curtis & MacCorquodale, 1990), it is generally the microsociological aspects of gender that are experienced as either restricting or liberating for women (McCall & Simmons, 1978; Millett, 1970; Oliker, 1989). Women's ability to achieve economic independence is a critical outcome of their socialization. Rapid social changes in modern industrial societies have made the attainment of basic economic means a necessity for women's survival (Rosen, 1989), and women must be able to meet many lifecycle crises (Ozawa, 1989; Peterson, 1989).

Knowledge of social change facilitates an assessment of the influence of gender on individual and social behavior (Wallace, 1989). Attitudes about women, as well as women's overt behavior, change through the generations (Roper & Labeff, 1977), and women's changing achievements are both a reflection and a product of those changing attitudes (Rosen, 1989).

IS THE FAMILY THE PRIMARY SITE OF WOMEN'S OPPRESSION?

The family is a prototype of community and society and frequently reflects a clearly marked sexual division of labor (Bradley, 1989; Coleman, 1988; Hiller & Philliber, 1986). Although these patterns can be modified radically by purposeful planning (Spiro, 1979), the organization and processes of family and household generally exhibit much inequality (Curtis, 1986).

Sociologists have conducted much research on the economic basis of family inequalities, frequently linking findings to the influence of capitalism (Zaretsky, 1976). However, lifecycle functions that families serve may be as strong an influence—or a stronger influence—in determining patterns of domestic behavior as are economic pressures (Foner & Kertzer, 1978).

Broad cultural influences, such as political ideologies and ethnic styles, infiltrate all families (Mason & Bumpass, 1975; Pescatello, 1973). The link between families and the workplace is also of considerable importance for women (Gutek 1985; Kessler-Harris, 1981, 1982; Matthaei, 1982). In modern industrial societies, it is particularly relevant for women to know how to cope with both traditional family responsibilities and their economic needs (Ozawa, 1989).

In order to be empowered, women must know how to value their varied contributions to the family and other social contexts (Reskin, 1988; Rosen, 1989). Although overburdened by family chores, women have shown that their overall functioning can be enhanced by assuming multiple roles (Sieber, 1974).

Women will be able to claim their freedom only when their choices are freed from the normative deep-emotional programming restricting their lives to meeting family responsibilities (Estep et al., 1977; Franks & McCarthy, 1989; McKinney & Sprecher, 1989). Attitudes have been changing demonstrably through the more recent generations (Linton, 1936; Turner, 1976), and women's subservience in the family (Marks, 1977) is being modified by their new values and adaptations (Oliker, 1989; Roper & Labeff, 1977).

CAN WOMEN BE EMPOWERED THROUGH RELIGION?

In most social classes and ethnic groups, families delegate to women the responsibility of children's religious training. Women are also frequently regarded as the moral leaders of the family, expressing unconditional love and support for all. The obligations and images associated with these traditional roles are onerous, and it is not surprising that women have been thought to be more oppressed by religion than freed by it (Hiller & Philliber, 1986).

One issue to raise in considering women's empowerment through religion is the extent to which women's traditional conditioning to perform the religious obligations can be reversed or modified. Assuming that women's required subservience to formal religious leadership, as well as their dutiful allegiance to family responsibilities, are learned, there must be ways to transform women's posture from being restricted to being empowered.

Women's subordination through major world religions is a worldwide phenomenon (Lindsay, 1980), and any change in the direction of empowerment is difficult to attain. As in other areas of women's subordination, unless women take deliberate steps to neutralize or reverse their original socialization and programming they will endlessly repeat the attitudes and behavior of women in past generations.

One way to resolve this dilemma may be for women to examine the emotional components of their religious beliefs. When women can be more objective about their own emotional functioning, as well as the cultural context in which they act, the chance of their making changes in their attitudes and behavior is enhanced (Franks & McCarthy, 1989).

An additional influence that comes into play in considering the difficulty of achieving women's empowerment through religion is the function of moral sanctions and moral standards. Unless women are able to evaluate the behavioral consequences of the religious beliefs they hold, they are unlikely to see any purpose or advantage to modifying those beliefs and, in fact, may insist that it would be immoral to examine their religious beliefs and practices with pragmatic objectives in mind.

CAN WOMEN BE FULFILLED THROUGH THEIR WORK?

In contemporary U.S. society, women's work is considered to be only work that is remunerated, rather than work that is conducted at home for no pay. This devaluation of women's work, and of the traditional roles of women, is a primary hindrance in attempts to accurately assess the contributions women make both inside and outside the home (Bose, Feldbera, & Sokoloff, 1987; Kessler-Harris, 1981; Levy, 1989; Lindsay, 1980).

Economic histories of women are beginning to acknowledge the total sum of economic functions that women perform (Matthaei, 1982; Rosen, 1989). Clearly, women's professional and occupational accomplishments outside their homes affect interaction in their families (Kessler-Harris, 1982; Mannehim, 1936; Zaretsky, 1976). A pattern repeated in the experience of women in all social classes and ethnic groups is that they tend to shoulder both full-time work outside the home and the work required to meet family responsibilities inside the home. This pattern is especially prevalent in modern industrial societies, in which the number of dual-earner families is increasing (Coleman, 1988; Curtis, 1986; Hiller & Philliber, 1986; Marks, 1977).

Although not all the consequences of these burdensome expectations are negative for women all of the time (Sieber, 1974), inevitably women are inordinately stressed in times of family crisis (Ozawa, 1989; Peterson, 1989). The changes needed to modify these pressures are so dramatic, however, that it may not be possible to resolve women's economic insecurities and family responsibilities without instigating a grand plan of cultural significance (Spiro, 1979).

Although some women are able to achieve advancement as equals in the workplace (Kanter, 1977), there is also much evidence to suggest that very little change is occurring in many of the established patterns of women's subordination as they work either outside or inside the home (Bradley, 1989; Gutek, 1985; Pescatello, 1973; Reskin, 1988). However, it appears that ideological changes—or changes in the values of women—may bring new sources of motivation that may shift some patterns of behavior (Mason & Bumpass, 1975). When women's stresses can be relieved through changes both in their orientations and in social structures, there will be a much greater probability that women will be fulfilled by work outside and inside the home.

ARE WOMEN IN OTHER COUNTRIES DIFFERENT FROM WOMEN IN THE UNITED STATES?

In world-system terms, women's subordination may be thought of as a type of social stratification (Della Fave, 1980). Worldwide patterns of capitalism also have an impact on the quality of women's lives in many different countries (Zaretsky, 1976). As in the United States, women's work in other cultural settings is frequently in domestic and agricultural home settings that are both hidden from view and socially unacknowledged (Bose et al., 1987; Levy, 1989; Linton, 1936).

Comparative sociological research provides a broad view of the regularities and repetitions in women's experience in different cultural and historical settings (Fonner & Kertzer, 1978; Gordon, 1988; Lindsay, 1980; Pescatello, 1973; Spiro, 1979). Data from research in a worldwide context increase the objectivity and representativeness of research findings from projects based in the United States (Gutek, 1985; Mason et al., 1976; Matthaei, 1982), and comparative research data also enhance and extend the resources needed for theory construction (Bradley, 1989; Curtis & MacCorquodale, 1990; McKinney & Sprecher, 1989; Ozawa, 1989).

As well as illuminating institutional similarities and differences, cross-cultural research findings show some of the variations in patterns of the self in different cultural settings (Turner, 1976). Interpretations of gender power phenomena link the interpersonal and social experiences of women, sometimes making political statements (Millett, 1970; Sanday, 1981), and feminism becomes an international phenomenon rather than staying limited as a national social movement (Malson, Barr, Wihl, & Wyer, 1989).

DOES FEMINISM INCREASE OR DECREASE WOMEN'S EMPOWERMENT?

The ideology of feminism is resisted by many women and men. Its values threaten the status quo and suggest revolutionary, pervasive changes that challenge cherished institutional traditions in families and religion (Dinnerstein, 1976; Fitzpatrick, 1990; Levy, 1989; Wallace, 1989). Feminism also suggests fundamental shifts in values at the level of the socialization and development of the young (Estep et al., 1977; Hewitt, 1990; Malson et al., 1989).

Feminism is often correlated with economic reform (Bose et al., 1987; Kessler-Harris, 1982; Mannheim, 1936). Although equal access to economic resources is of fundamental importance in securing equal rights (Lindsay, 1980; Linton, 1936; Peterson, 1989), women's achievements must be measured in a variety of ways (Reskin, 1988; Rosen, 1989).

The ideology of feminism is based on the central value of gender equality (Millett, 1970). Both an enhanced self-evaluation and social evaluation of women are central in bringing about an increased valuing of women and their work in society at large (Della Fave, 1980; Mason et al., 1976; Sydie, 1987). Furthermore, the support of women by women is crucial for achieving this objective (Oliker, 1989).

Feminism is useful for focusing research and interpersonal concerns (Marks, 1977; McCall & Simmons, 1978; McKinney & Sprecher, 1989). A full understanding of the social movement of feminism also facilitates the possibility of an adequate assessment of the degree and kind of change that is currently occurring in gender relations (Chafetz, 1990).

WHAT DOES WOMEN'S EMPOWERMENT ACHIEVE?

Women's empowerment involves changes at personal and societal levels (Berger, 1990; Fitzpatrick, 1990; Hewitt, 1990; Turner, 1976). Looking at transitions over the life course (Foner & Kertzer, 1978) and across the generations (Levy, 1989; Roper & Labeff, 1977), one can begin to see patterns of increase in female power but, at the same time, the relentless persistence of male dominance (Sanday, 1981).

Women's empowerment may mean little more than acknowledging the work women have always done (Kessler-Harris, 1981; Reskin, 1988). However, it also implies modes of communication and support between women (Oliker, 1989), as well as increases in women's awareness of their sexual objectification (Mason et al., 1976; Mason & Bumpass, 1975; Millett, 1970) and exploitation in work and family responsibilities (Bose et al., 1987; Bradley, 1989; Estep et al, 1977; Franks & McCarthy, 1989; Kessler-Harris, 1982; Marks, 1977).

One of the keys to women's empowerment in work (Kanter, 1977) and families (Hiller & Philliber, 1986) is the strengthening of identity at both interpersonal and social levels (Cohn, 1989; Della Fave, 1980; McCall & Simmons, 1978). The discipline of sociology is sufficiently broad and flexible to allow for a focus on both of these significant levels of analysis of women's empowerment (Gordon, 1988), thus enhancing the understanding of the consequences of women's empowerment.

Chapter 3

Self

For the purpose of understanding women's empowerment, self is defined as the essence of human uniqueness and originality—properties that underlie or transcend gender conditioning (Blumer, 1969; Cooley, 1962, 1964; Goffman, 1973; Mead, 1967). Although different ways of conceiving self are strongly influenced by gender, ethnic group, social class, religion, and other characteristics (Rosenberg, 1979), it is useful to think of basic humanness as a starting point for creating the conditions necessary for increased gender equality. This deliberate ambiguity in the examination of self allows for more androgynous options in defining gender and sex roles (Scott, 1982).

In order to know themselves fully, people must examine their group affiliations (Shibutani, 1955) and the different social settings in which they act on a daily basis (Glassner & Freedman, 1979). In fact, it may be only in the context of male patriarchies that people are able to understand certain aspects of women's self, such as women's definitions of personal limitations and possibilities (Wollstonecraft, 1982). The degree of women's integration in mainstream society also may be a primary condition of their physical, mental, and emotional health, as well as their everyday functioning (Durkheim, 1966).

A study of the evolution of human behavior necessarily includes an examination of the evolution of the self (Alland, 1967; Bowen, 1978; Hall, 1983; Kerr & Bowen, 1988). Particular kinds of self—those that are more or less differentiated from other selves—can be thought of as generating or expressing characteristic patterns of behavior.

Some general or overall changes in human capacities, such as increases in class or race consciousness, may be due more to historical awareness than to genetic mutation. As women become more aware of the role they have played in the growth of civilization (Beard, 1971), they become more inclined to align themselves with other women to bring about further changes (Smelser, 1962). However, when women maintain a restricted life-style through societal emphases on their domestic loyalties and responsibilities, they are fearful of venturing far from their familiar, traditional dependencies (Dowling, 1982).

In a rapidly changing society, such as the United States, most people absorb a wide range of contradictory beliefs. People become contemporary in spite of themselves, because homogeneous traditional beliefs no longer prepare them adequately for routine everyday stresses in their lives (Luckmann, 1967). When women move beyond their family loyalties to pursue their deepest interests (Gerson, 1985; Hall, 1979), they are compelled to absorb some modern beliefs to cope with the changes in their lives and to establish necessarily more meaningful allegiances with other women (Diaz-Diocaretz & Zavala, 1985).

Personal relationships are sources for growth of self, as well as for limits on options (Cancian, 1987). People generally deal with friendships more freely than with their families (Bell, 1981), although it is through interaction with families that people grow most of all (Bowen, 1978). By entering into paid work, women frequently question more fully what it is they consider important (Davies & Esseveld, 1982) and what their beliefs about reality really are (Randour, 1987). Self is defined more clearly through this kind of scrutiny of values and through the additional contacts made in the work setting. Questioning and interacting with families and the wider society empower self. Who women are and who they believe they are influence their behavior (Mead, 1967), and their value choices about what they do with their lives have a direct impact on others as well as on themselves (Hall, 1990a).

Although women cannot indefinitely artificially construct or manipulate self to their advantage, they can come to realize that their life histories intersect with society's history and that their personal decisions have consequences for the largest arenas. Women reflect society, and at the same time they create their own social conditions (Mills, 1967). It is this challenge and responsibility to meaningfully combine their beliefs about self with their knowledge of wider society that strengthens and empowers women. Women's roles are modified and sometimes transformed in the interplay between women's self-definition and their participation in society.

LIFE HISTORIES

In this section, three life histories illustrate how women empower self. Clinical sociology, and especially identity empowerment theory, suggest strategies and techniques for crisis intervention and therapeutic direction. In order to capture the broad picture of life changes made by these women, however, attention is given here only to the particular circumstances of the three women and their decisionmaking, rather than to the therapeutic and research methodologies used in collecting the data.

Rosemary

Rosemary is a married, middle-class, white woman who has two children aged 2 and 5 years old. She has professional training in nursing, but has been reluctant to work for pay because her husband is able to support her and her children. It was only when she suffered from severe depressions that she had to ask herself whether she was living her life as fully and as meaningfully as she could. Eventually Rosemary came to see that depression was common among educated, middle-class, white women confined to the house with domestic responsibilities. As a result, she felt less isolated and began to realize that she need not conform to others' expectations that she be a wife and mother at home. Finally, she chose to continue her career in nursing.

It was hard for Rosemary to make satisfactory arrangements for the care of her children because her husband would not change his working hours. She arranged to trade babysitting time with a neighborhood friend who felt fulfilled staying at home with her children. She made a work schedule based on this friend's cooperation. As she had reentered the work force on a part-time basis, this informal exchange worked satisfactorily.

Rosemary soon felt benefits from having a new kind of work life that took her out of the home. Although she did not get much emotional or domestic support from her husband, he did not criticize her verbally. Because of the increased family income, they were able to afford to hire household help, so stresses related to home care were alleviated.

One benefit of Rosemary's changed perception of herself as a mother working outside as well as inside the home was that she gained self-esteem. She enjoyed parenting more than when she was at home all the time, and she did not try to maintain the same housekeeping standards she had before she returned to her nursing career. She was overjoyed to have a more meaningful life.

If Rosemary had not been able to see herself as successfully coping with the different burdens and responsibilities that her new work brought her, she would not have been able to make the changes easily. The pain she had experienced through her depressions gave her good cause to break out of her former restricted mode of living. She also was able to take the action necessary to make this change, because she had previously noticed that whenever she was with people outside her immediate family she felt more challenged and more ful-filled.

Today, Rosemary is able to communicate effectively to her husband that continuing to work outside the home and to make other changes are important to her. She is able to enjoy her husband's company more because her strength-ened sense of self connects her to the wider society and allows her to transcend many of the irritations and burdens of necessary parenting and domestic chores.

Grace

Grace is a single, black woman who is about 30 years old. She is a talented singer and an accomplished scholar of music history. As a girl, she struggled to educate herself and to find the time and energy to cultivate her voice. Grace is an only child who was raised by her mother alone; she saw relatively little of her father while she was growing up. She had several relatives living close to her and her mother, however, so she benefited from a great deal of family support as a youngster.

Grace is fortunate in that her mother trained her to be very independent. Her relatives gave her the freedom she needed to be herself, as well as the companionship she craved.

Grace is a religious young woman. She is active in a Protestant church community, and she has many friends in the congregation. Although most of her peers have children, Grace decided that at this time she prefers to have a college teaching career rather than to have a family of her own. She spends much of her time on weekends with friends or relatives who have young chil-dren, so she is with children as much as she wants to be at present.

Grace goes to many parties, and she enjoys working with men at her col-lege and in her church community. She has several men friends, but no passion-ate relationship that could lead to marriage or a live-in arrangement. She has decided that at this stage of her life an intense romantic involvement would detract from her strong desire to pursue career goals.

Grace is very level-headed. She is a fine example of personal strength for younger members of her family. Although she experienced a tough beginning to life, perhaps because of those very hardships Grace is skilled in meeting her own personal and career needs and in being supportive to others. She gains advantages from her own openness and helpfulness to those who are emotion-ally close to her.

Grace has a rosy career ahead of her. Although she may not achieve star-dom as a singer, her care in preparing herself as a college educator means that her long-range career goals will give her a direction to pursue for many years to come.

Janet

Janet is a lower-class, white, retired shop assistant who is widowed. She lives alone in a small city apartment, and her five children have their homes at least 100 miles away from her.

Initially on retirement, Janet found her life very empty. Because she had no family at home and no daily contacts from her retail work, time hung heavily on her hands. Fortunately, she made the decision to fill her days with activities she enjoys.

Janet has six grandchildren whom she rarely sees. One way she has increased meaning in her life is to visit them. Both she and her grandchildren benefit from these contacts, which she initiates.

Although Janet is not a religious person, she attends church regularly in order to have more contact with other people. She is a Roman Catholic, so there are many services and rituals from which she can choose. Janet is active in some church social activities, and at least once a week she visits sick parishioners in a local hospital.

Janet's sense of well-being has increased since she began to take her grandparenting responsibilities more seriously through her personal visits. She has also gained a great deal from sharing her time with those who are ill.

In some respects, Janet's life is now more comfortable and relaxed than it was when she had to endure the rigid grind of a dull job. She is coping with her retirement transition admirably through her varied activities, and she now has more friends than she ever had before. Janet is especially close to some of the widows she has met while attending church.

As Janet becomes more settled in her new life-style, and is less emotionally needy, her children visit her fairly often. She is more at peace with her role as a parent than she was at earlier times. Due to their small incomes and many family responsibilities, Janet and her husband had been in relatively dire economic straits for long periods of time.

Janet's children ask her many questions about the past. As she explains the details of their family's history to her children, her life takes on new meaning. Even Janet's most rebellious and emotionally distant children have visited her. Some of this animosity was more related to their father than to Janet, and now that Janet is alone they are able to come to terms with their conflicts of the past.

Janet's strength lies in her openness to change in her advancing years. This is not a new pattern for her; over the years she has consistently been an imaginative and resourceful person. What is new is that Janet no longer pays much attention to others' expectations of her, or to the stereotypes attributed to older people. Her "careless" attitude serves Janet well, and she has become her own kind of rebel as she deals effectively and expansively with what are all too frequently thought of as unavoidable or necessary restrictions of old age.

ANALYSIS AND INTERPRETATION

Of the three women described above, Grace has the clearest and strongest sense of self. She has a specific long-range purpose in her life, and is acting deliberately and consistently toward achieving this purpose. She has chosen her goal of a career in singing and music history education in a remarkably independent way. She is the only person in her family to have effectively achieved so much through education.

Another of Grace's strengths is that she has effective support networks to which she also contributes. The continuities in her exchanges and interaction with her family and her church community stabilize her single life and allow her to be professionally mobile.

Grace is as deliberate and thoughtful about her personal life as she is about her career development and advancement. She has secure female and male friendships, and she has made a firm decision not to be married at this time. This decision flows from her prior decision to take her career in college teaching seriously.

Rosemary is strengthening self, but very soon may have to make more serious decisions about her career in nursing. She has successfully relieved her symptoms of severe depression, which is no mean accomplishment, but she has yet to stabilize her life as Grace has done. Perhaps this is innately more difficult for Rosemary to do, as she is both a wife and a mother of young children.

Because Rosemary has felt so many benefits from making the changes she has made so far, it could be predicted that she would continue in this vein as the years go by. At present, however, there are a great deal of transient and make-shift arrangements in her everyday life.

Rosemary cannot count on her husband's support in the essentials of child care, and she cannot easily afford the kind of child care she would need to have if she were to return to nursing full-time. It is perhaps to Rosemary's advantage, however, that she is communicating effectively with her husband. She gets some remote support and interest from him, as well as some financial assistance in rearing their children. As of now the marriage itself is not becoming visibly stressed by Rosemary's working outside of the home. In fact, her marriage is benefiting from her expanded interests and increased contacts at the hospital, as is her parenting. She is making the most of a difficult situation.

Janet's situation is more similar to Rosemary's than it is to Grace's. Janet has spent a life time adapting to others' needs, and it has been difficult for her to start acting independently. In the presence of this inhibition and her reluctance to make changes in her life, Janet has had to adapt to the shifts created by her retirement.

Like Rosemary, Janet is just beginning to focus on self and live with and within the decisions she makes for herself alone. She is doing well in her efforts to neutralize some of her past conditioning, and she is creating a stronger support group than she has ever had before. Her improved contact with her children and grandchildren is a very vital support, and she is not a needy or dependent participant in these relationships.

In some respects, Janet's decisions have the potential of being more permanent than Rosemary's changes. Janet is not considering having a career, and she no longer has parenting responsibilities. She wants to stay in her city apartment, so she can adjust more easily to these new patterns than Rosemary can.

Neither Rosemary nor Janet is as single-minded and goal-directed as Grace, which indicates that they are not as aware of what they want to do with their lives as is Grace. However, as each woman defines self in the context of different family, work, and social contexts, self is empowered. It is only when symptoms of depression or loneliness are not confronted or examined that self is diminished rather than empowered.

CHOICES

A focus on self—a fundamental aspect or initial stage of women's empowerment—gives rise to the need to make particular choices. Although women may not make all of these choices, the kinds of dilemmas described below need to be addressed sooner or later.

1 Women must choose to put their own interests first in relationship issues. Automatically putting others first is a conditioned reaction that ultimately hurts women.

2 Women must choose independence over dependence, especially in emotional and financial matters. It is particularly difficult for women to meet their own emotional needs, but all romance distorts reality.

3 The choice to define self clearly implies having sufficient awareness of the values women cherish most. Often women are not aware of their choice of their deepest values until those values are threatened.

4 Empowerment results from being aware of the choices that one has at any time and in any situation. Awareness of choices can be painful, because being aware increases responsibility for behavior.

5 The choice to be empowered implies the choice to act constructively and cooperatively with others. Empowered action does not impinge on the rights of others.

6 The choice to be a self necessitates letting go of false images and the effort to please other people. Being a true and real self means that all hypocrisies must go; only the facts of who a woman is can remain.

GENERALIZATIONS

Living from self necessitates having a working knowledge of the pressures society imposes on women, which prevent women from being who they are or who they want to be. Women in all social classes and in all ethnic groups are restricted from being themselves by society's need for them to function in major commitment roles, such as motherhood.

Some generalizations can be made about women's particularly acute struggle for autonomy. Both women and men function from self, so some of these patterns also apply to men.

1 Women tend to focus on relationships rather than on goals, so their energies easily become dissipated in situations where they put others before themselves. Goal-directed behavior is more efficient and more satisfying—for women as well as for men.

2 When women direct their actions toward becoming more autonomous, they predictably meet resistance from others, especially those who are emotionally closest to them. Women cannot count on the support of their significant others in making the journey of empowerment.

3 It is difficult for women to clarify the values and beliefs they hold dearest to them, even if those values and beliefs are not in their own best interests. Neither women nor men are usually aware of their own values and beliefs, unless they make a deliberate effort to know themselves.

4 There is no time when one can afford not to be aware of self. Being a self means being vigilant and prepared to act independently at all times.

5 Being a self necessitates being sufficiently free neither to conform to nor to rebel against others' expectations. Women are their own selves when they are autonomous in relation to stereotypes and images of women.

6 Empowerment is synonymous with the growth and maturation of self. Women strengthen self by being more of a self than they have been able to be in their past.

PROPOSITIONS

Propositions about self and society, which apply particularly to women, are listed below. These propositions are tentative, but can be substantiated to some degree of satisfaction with life history data.

1 The more effort women invest in understanding self, the more they will be empowered. Being a self necessitates investing a great deal of hard work and emotional energy and being persistent.

2 The more women deviate from others' expectations, the more their actions will be resisted by those same others. Women's families and friends have vested interests in maintaining the status quo, so when women change their functioning others try to restore what they perceive to be the previous equilibrium.

3 The more women remain centered in self, the more effectively they will be able to take charge of their lives in all situations. When a woman acts from her true and real self, her behavior is much more effective than when she has no clear source of her actions.

4 To the extent that a woman is empowered, that woman will have a strong self. Self is the base from which all her actions flow, and the source of her deepest and most meaningful values.

5   The less attention women pay to what other people think women ought to do, the more they get a sense of what their true direction is. Sometimes women discern what it is they really want to do by eliminating their conditioning and reflecting on their sense of nothingness.

6   When women are destructive to others, they also hurt themselves. Sometimes women unwittingly hurt themselves most of all when they do not live their lives fully from self. Women's distortion of self is inevitably followed by destructive acts to self and others.

Chapter 4

Gender

Gender is defined by patterns of learned behavior that are considered appropriate either for women alone or for men alone. Historically, most values and expectations for women's behavior have been articulated in relation to men, rather than independently in terms related to women as a group (Lengermann & Wallace, 1985; Richardson, 1988). In fact, it is frequently difficult for both women and men to think of women as being culturally distinct from men (Martyna, 1980), or as having destinies and goals that go beyond those defined by men (Beard, 1971; Morgan, 1982).

Much gender behavior is compartmentalized into stereotyped roles, which are artificially polarized or contrived to be complementary to that of the other gender. In many vital respects women are segregated from the world of men (Bernard, 1981), and women's delegated work and traditional responsibilities frequently confine them to the domestic sphere (Oakley, 1975, 1976). When women work outside of the home, the division of labor in factories, corporations, and other organizational settings shows persistent patterns of segregation (Reskin & Hartman, 1986). Although some explanations of these trends give weight to the quality of women's motivations (Horner, 1972), clinical sociologists and other sociologists suggest that social structures, such as avenues of access to resources, keep women in segregated and subordinate roles (Glassner & Freedman, 1979; Weitzman, 1979).

Even in scientific investigations about the nature of women's lives and cultural experiences, women and their characters are frequently defined through their sexual functions (Freud, 1982; Morgan, 1982). However, recent social and cultural changes have created a wider consensus on possibilities for seeing women in a variety of ways. The view that women have more opportunities available to them than bearing and raising children is increasingly accepted (Intons-Peterson, 1988). It is also increasingly acknowledged that women have distinctive values and priorities and that their moral decisions are based on criteria that are different from men's (Gilligan, 1982).

Genetic and learned social and emotional differences between women and men lead to numerous challenges in relationships. The contemporary felt need for meaningful companionship between women and men has increased people's interests in personal growth (Cancian, 1987). Being a woman today no longer implies the automatic subordination that was common in the United States and Europe even as recently as the 1960s (Beauvoir, 1974).

Emerging new patterns in gender relations may be thought of as a new stage in human evolution (Alland, 1967). Recent thinking about women may lead to behavior that will not revert to former ways of doing things (Aga, 1984; Andersen, 1988), although many established patterns in gender relations persist without interruption.

Women are frequently thought of and experienced by men as threats to men's status (Hays, 1964). However, statistics on physical and emotional violence and abuse between women and men show that women are overwhelmingly the victims in female-male conflicts and not the oppressors (Brownmiller, 1975; Finkelhor & Gelles, 1983; Flowers, 1987; Hindberg, 1988; Straus, Gelles, & Steinmetz, 1980). It is more accurate to postulate that women are their own worst enemies because self-destructive behavior tends to flow from the actualization of women's wishes and fantasies about what it is to be "real" women (Chernin, 1981).

Women and men are beginning to recognize that women have their own kinds of sexual needs (Coward, 1984), and that they are entitled to aspire to and exercise power (Lipmen-Blumen, 1984). Clinical data suggest that the more traditional, narrowly defined, polarized, gender-specific behavior is unhealthy for both women and men, and that androgynous models of gender behavior are more viable as ideals for the optimal functioning of women and men. On a social level, beliefs in a "right to be human" through equal sex roles (Scott, 1982) are beginning to replace the traditional myths and fantasies that perpetuate and reinforce women's dependence on men and their resistance to becoming independent (Dowling, 1982).

Established definitions of human nature (Cooley, 1964) need to be redefined by adding the accumulated new knowledge about women. Similarly, a deeper understanding of minority women's experiences must be used to challenge and reformulate assumptions about what constitutes women's experiences and behavior (Staples, 1973).

In examining the interplay between women's awareness and the social order (Mead, 1967), new trends and precedents must be identified. When new knowledge about gender can be linked to the humanistic concern for equity, new principles will emerge. For example, equality will be accepted by more people when the concept of the comparable worth of women and men is understood more fully. Women and men perform different economic and social roles in society, but in many respects parity between these contributions can be demonstrated (Steinberg & Haignere, 1984).

Another area in which gender must be defined more equally is that of religion and spirituality. Women are beginning to experiment with their own religious needs, and to develop new forms and rituals of spirituality. As women's spirituality is developed, new views and ideas will necessarily emerge to influence, and perhaps contradict, established ways of doing things (Christ, 1983; Christ & Plaskow, 1979). In all the institutional orders of society, and perhaps especially in the area of religion and spirituality, gender perspectives have the potential for being bases or sources of formulations of new paradigms. These deeper and more accurate ways to understand gender experiences will serve to build more representative, meaningful, and reliable knowledge (Kuhn, 1970).

LIFE HISTORIES

Three examples of women who question their gender identities are given below. Emphasis is given to how each woman chooses to actively shape her gender identity to effectively avoid being restricted by traditional patriarchal definitions and expectations.

In order to facilitate the making of comparisons and contrasts between their experiences, each life history summarizes the original data collected from the three women. Directions taken in the women's empowerment are similar in some basic respects, however, in that empowerment necessarily involves an opening up of women's conventionally restricted worlds and responsibilities. The particular details appearing in the descriptions are purposely selected to illustrate some of the variations in ways in which empowerment is expressed on individual, social, or political levels.

Ruth

Ruth is a young, Orthodox Jewish woman who was trained—by family influences and through her religion—to accept traditional gender differences as the foundation of her social life. However, during adolescence, she experimented with behaviors not accepted within this learned version of reality. She rebelled against her parents' and brothers' expectations of her and tried to live according to her own values.

Ruth realized that her rebellion allowed her to broaden her awareness and deepen her understanding of what it meant to her to be a woman. Her formerly rather fixed ideas about womanhood were changed through her active questioning and testing of the expectations of those who were emotionally closest to her.

As a young woman, Ruth is now open to many more options for her future life than her mother was when she was young. She has decided not to plan marriage for the near future and is pursuing a demanding career in physics. Having this challenging professional goal clearly in mind, she is able to avoid becoming overly involved in the many restrictive dependencies and relationship interests in her everyday family life.

Ruth's persistent focus on ambitious goals and her expansive career possibilities keep her from being trapped in a domestic role, as her mother and grandmothers had been. Her gender identity is not something she takes for granted. Her challenges to others' gender expectations are an adventure of discovery for her, and the skills she gains from these challenges serve as resources for the strengthening of her professional and personal talents.

May

May is a retired, black school teacher. She is widowed and looks after her older sister, who is housebound because of a chronic illness. May's only child, a son, lives several hundreds of miles away from her, and she rarely sees him. Her son is divorced and has no children.

May keeps active by undertaking a variety of daily activities outside of her home. Her sister needs May home in the evenings, but in the daytime May works part-time as a consultant-administrative assistant in the school system. Although this position does not give May much pay or status, it gives her an opportunity to use the talents and professional experience she has acquired over the years. May is the first woman in her family to successfully pursue a career.

May's mother held several part-time jobs and retired at an early age. Her health was not good and, like May's sister, she became housebound. She was widowed shortly after her retirement; leading a quiet life at home seemed to be the most appropriate thing for her to do, especially as she did not need to work outside of the home to keep her expenses paid. May's mother lived modestly and received social security.

May had to work hard to maintain her independence. Family and community pressures moved toward limiting May's activities rather than toward keeping her active in her professional work.

May is highly motivated by her own philosophy, which has served her well throughout her adult life. She feels indebted to the community, because she received a good education. Although May still receives some pay for her current work in education, she feels she would need to do volunteer work if her paid position were terminated. She wants to contribute her services so much that she is unaware that this desire enhances her health. She gives to others for the love of giving, and her generous actions and altruistic attitude keep her world open and sufficiently large to enable her to meet stresses in her life vibrantly and meaningfully.

Joanne

As a young girl, Joanne dreamed of being a perfect wife and mother. She married a man she met in college and soon settled into a suburban life-style. She made decisions rather automatically, without asking herself what she really wanted to do with her life.

Joanne could not understand why she was not happy with her marriage and life at home with her two children. Over time she grew restless and frustrated with the long hours of being alone with her young children. Her husband travelled a great deal, and she could not depend on him for companionship. Because Joanne experienced so much pain in her loneliness, she started to socialize with her friends in local restaurants in the evenings. Because she lived in a small town, this was easy for her to do, and, for a while, the activity outside of her home made her feel better.

Before long, however, Joanne realized that she had to build her own life. She knew she must concern herself less with trying to be two parents to her children, or with trying to compensate for her husband's inadequate companionship.

As part of her effort to put her own life together, Joanne made a decision to work in her older sister's real estate business in a neighboring town. She proceeded to do what she could on a part-time basis to learn the mechanics of her sister's business, and to earn her own real estate license.

When her children were a little older, Joanne left her sister's company and started her own retail party goods business close to her home. She was successful at her new business from the beginning, and soon accumulated enough income to make it possible for her to leave her husband. Joanne has become so busy with her business and with her continued parenting responsibilities that she has no time left for socializing with her former friends. As she conducts business, however, she has made and continues to make new supportive women friends who are very nurturing of her in times of crisis and stress.

ANALYSIS AND INTERPRETATION

Each of these women had to struggle in order to define her gender identity and gender role. Gender identity has a strong influence on all women's behavior. Women's abilities to learn, make decisions, and modify what they take for granted depend on what they believe it means to be women.

May is most able to do what she wants without immediate pressure and resistance from others. It would have been very easy for her to succumb to family expectations, however, and to the patterns of the past experiences of her mother and sister in leading a narrowly restricted life. May is exemplary in that her empowered action throughout her adult life is built on a philosophy that she has created for herself. In continuing her professional life, May was fortunate to have only her sister to deal with in her personal life. Although her son's distance made her lonely, she was relieved not to be at his beck and call. She also had the freedom to arrange for neighbors to stay with her sister if she wanted to get away for a while.

Ruth was initially in the most difficult position of all three of these women. It is especially difficult for women to grow up to be themselves in families where standards and customs are strongly reinforced by traditional religious beliefs. Orthodox Judaism is a fairly closed belief system. As such, it creates an uncomfortably intense emotional climate in which children must learn what the world and reality are all about, as well as who they are and what is expected of them.

As a consequence of her early training, it is doubtful that Ruth could have claimed emotional independence without rebelling. There is no easy way in which she could have modified her position within the family's narrowly restricted standards and expectations without appearing to be an outsider, as well as a threat to their beliefs and values. Ruth was impressively creative in channeling her energies toward career goals and a single social life, as she learned to stop responding to her family's emotional demands.

In contrast to May and Ruth, Joanne has to deal with her husband and two small children in order to create an emotionally and economically satisfying life for herself. Joanne made relatively rapid progress in empowering herself after she realized that typical suburban life was not for her. Her discomfort with this conventional life-style led her to question and clarify her values. She was able to make effective changes in her life by focusing on her own needs as well as those of her children. As Joanne became more independent, her children benefited. They too became more independent, because Joanne had given them a strong role model with whom to identify.

Joanne's divorce and economic success flowed from her confidence in her own competence, and from her taking the opportunities that were available to her in the small town where she lived. The immediate gains she received from her business were very satisfying to her. Her economic success strengthened her self-respect, and she enjoyed being able to provide a comfortable home for her children.

Ruth, May, and Joanne came to define their gender expectations in ways that contrast with traditional and conventional stereotypes. They each had to examine gender values in order to change their lives and adapt effectively. To the extent that they behaved automatically and followed their conditioning, their choices could have proved hazardous for them. They needed to err on the side of rejecting traditional gender stereotypes, rather than acquiesce and accept those stereotypes without question in order to function autonomously and effectively.

Empowerment is a slow growth process through which each woman becomes able to see the broader picture of her life and to live more consistently according to her values. When others' resistance to these changes are dealt with, women's well-being and satisfaction are increased.

CHOICES

Reflections about gender enable women to know that there are critical choices to be made about how they define themselves as women. Some of the dilemmas that must be dealt with in making gender role choices are listed below.

1 In order to be true to self and gender, women must choose to examine their deepest values. It is not enough for women to think of themselves merely as women. They need to know what kind of women they are, and whether they choose—or want to choose—traditional or modern values to express themselves.

2 Choosing to be true to gender does not mean that women should succumb to the gender stereotypes that abound in society. A close examination of women's stereotypes reveals many contradictions. Women must choose their freedom to define what gender means to them above all else.

3 The choice to define gender expansively suggests more life-enhancing consequences than the choice to accept restrictive interpretations of gender. Growth comes through experimenting with choices to broaden the bases of thinking and action.

4 It is supremely important for women to choose to be honest with themselves. Women must face the facts of their oppression and shoulder the responsibility to make changes in their lives. If they depend on others to make those choices for them, the resulting changes will not be real or long lasting.

5 When women choose to define gender for themselves, the source of their actions becomes more consolidated. When women are not sure what it means to be women, their behavior is scattered and ineffective.

6 Choosing to examine in depth the family programming that created their beliefs about being women is a significant stage in women's freeing themselves from others' expectations for them as women. When women see the origins of their values, they can distance themselves from those values more effectively and take increasing control over their own choices.

GENERALIZATIONS

Women become freer to make their own choices without being influenced by complex social influences when they see those influences and associated interdependencies clearly. Gender stereotypes inevitably restrict women. Thus the greatest rewards come from understanding the breadth and variety of gender possibilities that exist. Some patterns and tendencies in gender definitions are outlined below to demonstrate more fully the broader picture of gender.

1   Gender expectations are first internalized in the family. It is essential to understand family dynamics and expectations as sources of gender socialization in order to recognize and deal with the pressures to conform to specific gender patterns of behavior.

2   Gender values and beliefs tend to be sharply polarized between women and men. However, life history data show that more stable and secure women combine female and male values, rather than become extremely feminine in their beliefs.

3   Internalized gender standards can be changed at any time. Women learn their gender behavior. Therefore, with consistent effort, these patterns in women's personal and public lives can be modified. Learned gender values do not seal the fate of women.

4   Gender expectations vary dramatically between social classes and ethnic groups, as well as in different historical and cultural settings. However, similarities can be gleaned by focusing on functioning areas of women's lives, such as their families, religion, and work.

5   The whole of society can be thought of as being organized on the basis of gender. The division of labor between the genders is so fundamental to occupational hierarchies that there are two economies—one for each gender—rather than one well-integrated economy.

6   The most basic way to accomplish changes in gender expectations in society at large is through the early socialization of children. It is not that communicating the content of particular roles for women and men is essential to constructive socialization, but rather that it is essential to create conditions that will foster the autonomy and independence of both girls and boys.

PROPOSITIONS

By concentrating on one or two aspects of the gender situation of women, women's vision of life as a whole can be deepened and sharpened. It is difficult to see the whole picture all of the time, but it is important to try to see the connections between the complex interdependencies that influence women's lives.

The propositions below suggest links between one or two variables in order to understand gender more fully. The micro- and macrospheres of women's lives also must be considered in light of these associations.

1   Women who become more autonomous in their families automatically loosen their gender definitions. By claiming their independence from significant others, women are able to be independent in defining gender.

2 Denominational religions tend to support and reinforce conservative stereotypes of gender. By examining their religious beliefs, women can select those values that allow them to stay within religious traditions and, at the same time, to have freedom in gender values and beliefs.

3 The more rigid and polarized women are in their gender values and beliefs, the more at risk they will be for mental and emotional disorders. Health and stamina are derived from the more androgynous definitions of gender that women can create through their thoughts, feelings, and behavior.

4 Gender is at the core of women's values and beliefs. It is difficult to formulate a clear idea of self without associating it with gender. This closeness of self and gender in women's experiences suggests the supreme importance of gender influence in giving direction and meaning to women's lives, even though they may not be aware of that influence.

5 Women's support for each other clarifies their understanding of what gender is in their lives. Women see themselves in each others' experiences, and they can assess the importance of the influence of gender in their life chances when they hear and see those influences in other women's lives.

6 Gender is eternal and universal. Making historical and cross-cultural comparisons of women's experiences is essential to increasing their objectivity and to broadening and deepening their understanding of what it means to be a woman here and now.

Chapter 5

Women and Families

Many authors suggest that women are oppressed through their family responsibilities (Caute, 1967; Chodorow, 1978, 1989; Engels, 1970; Mitchell, 1975; Schaef, 1985). Women's early socialization frequently results in restricting their lives to domestic milieus (Blumer, 1969). Moreover, women's lack of power in decisionmaking within and outside families (Blau, 1967) limits their everyday activities, even within families.

Although social changes have modified some of these established patterns of behavior, it is frequently hypothesized that what happens in families in large part determines life chances (Bowen, 1978; Hall, 1983; Kerr & Bowen, 1988). Furthermore, it is very difficult for women to change family pressures and expectations themselves, even when they are highly motivated to do so (Hall, 1979). To the extent that women identify with their mothers and grandmothers (Friday, 1977), this cycle of inhibitions and controls on women's activities is perpetuated from generation to generation (Larsson & Olson, 1988).

Due to the significance of family relations for everyone's well-being and functioning, some feminists advocate more awareness of family concerns in the formulation of legislation and in establishing community support programs

(Friedan, 1981). The most personal spheres of family interaction—the two- and three-person interdependencies between spouses or between parents and child— are among the strongest influences on women's perceptions of themselves and on their orientation to others and the world.

The history of children (Aries, 1965) and the modern welfare state (Dencik, 1989) suggests that women's traditional responsibilities should be shared by spouses, families, and the state in order to ensure the most effective parenting for all. In some situations, neighborhood supports and friendship networks (Bell, 1981; Bott, 1957; Hill, 1972) are effective supplemental or substitute resources for fathers or mothers (Aytac, 1990; Haas, 1981; Ross, 1987).

The newest predominant economic family structure—the dual-earner family—tends to reflect more egalitarian values than the nuclear family, where only the husband worked outside of the home, and traditional hierarchical families (Aldous, 1982; Hood, 1983). However, all too often in dual-earner families, women assume not only work responsibilities outside the home, but also the larger part of domestic and parenting responsibilities inside the home (Feinstein, 1979). It has been predicted, but not substantiated, that as more women develop careers, there will be increased reciprocity in spouses' sharing of everyday family tasks (Pleck, 1985; Rapoport & Rapoport, 1971, 1976). This mutuality would be based on a shared belief in the importance of being human, rather than on following the dictates of conventionally polarized gender roles (Scott, 1982).

Women's well-being and autonomy frequently derive from their abilities to control economic resources, generally through working outside the home (Feinstein, 1979). Women increasingly forge personal and social identities through their work outside of the home, as well as inside the home (Davies & Esseveld, 1982). A corollary of this is that women in poverty, especially those who are single parents, are essentially victims of an economy that is not hospitable to women's needs to work outside the home and their family responsibilities (Pearce, 1983; Rosaldo & Lamphere, 1974; Weitzman, 1985; Westwood, 1985; Wilson, 1980). Dilemmas of this kind make it very difficult for all women to make major life decisions about their families and work preferences (Gerson, 1985), especially as it is no longer economically and socially feasible to accept the traditional housewife role (Bergmann, 1981).

Traditional divisions of labor patterns and their characteristic work conditions dominate women's lives and their families in countries throughout the world, as well as in all ethnic groups (Frazier, 1939; Glick, 1985; Goode, 1963; London, 1985; Staples, 1985). Contrasting cultural values, as well as varied economic conditions, clearly define expectations for women and the major dimensions of their everyday realities (Kluckhohn & Strodtbeck, 1961).

Both women's individual growth (Cancian, 1987) and their self-destructiveness (Chernin, 1981) have been shown to be strongly influenced by their family responsibilities and dependencies. It is also recognized that violence is centered in families, and that women are most frequently the victims of that violence (Finkelhor & Gelles, 1983; Gelles, 1979; Hindberg, 1988; Straus et al., 1980). Women's empowerment neutralizes some of the life-threatening trends that emerge within families.

Institutional structures have been useful in meeting some needs of women. Welfare programs meet some needs (Waerness & Ringen, 1987), although over-all value changes are necessary preconditions for women's long-term increased effectiveness (Trost, 1984). Traditional religion may provide support for some women who are trying to cope with family responsibilities (Burdick, 1990; Shehan et al., 1990), but the development of women's own spirituality and their expressions of this spirituality can both support and motivate women to tran-scend their restricted conditions. Women's spirituality can orient them toward broader spheres of activity and more fulfillment.

LIFE HISTORIES

Three life histories that follow illustrate how family connectedness can em-power women to pursue their lives more autonomously. Also, in some in-stances, informal friendship networks are effective substitutes for family, essen-tially serving the same support function as extended families.

In each example, the women have reached beyond the traditional nuclear family and expanded their support systems to include additional relatives or friends. The optimal support families can give goes beyond the small, frag-mented units of kin that have been thought of as families in the Western experi-ence.

Faye

Faye is a young, black, single mother. She has no contact with the father of her son. She never knew her own father and, therefore, is fairly well prepared to raise her son alone, as her mother raised her. Faye is fortunate to have relatives and friends who live close by, and who are willing to help her meet the daily demands of child care.

Faye is active in the community life of her church. She participates in a parenting group and spends much time with other young mothers. With her mother's encouragement, she enrolled in community college courses to pursue a degree program.

Faye has effectively created an extended family for herself and her son. These kin and kin substitutes give her sufficient support so that she is able to better herself economically and more adequately provide for her son. It appears that it is Faye's respect for the importance of family that motivates her to keep her neighborhood connections strong. She reciprocates others' child-care help by looking after elderly relatives and sick neighbors, as well as children, especially during weekend times that might otherwise be lonely for her.

Faye also helps with family parties in neighbors' homes at holiday times. Because she takes her son with her on these occasions, he meets more people and is becoming accustomed to a wider variety of social situations than Faye's own life offers him.

Faye's family and substitute family empower her. These deep-seated, emotionally significant contacts increase her autonomy and provide the support she needs as a young, single parent.

Rita

Rita is a middle-aged Argentinean woman who married young; she has five adult children. Rita worked extremely hard to support her children when they were young. She did housework in other people's homes to supplement her husband's income as a janitor. In spite of being the younger sister of two older brothers, Rita has been able to maintain her independence in family decision-making situations over the years. Although her parents are no longer living, and all her oldest relatives are still in Argentina, she has frequent contact with her two older brothers who live in the United States, as well as contact with her husband's family and her own children's families.

Rita has returned to Argentina infrequently since her emigration to the United States 30 years ago. Fifteen years ago, she visited her mother before her mother died. She went back to Argentina to sort out her father's belongings after his unexpected death 5 years ago. Her contacts with relatives in Argentina give her a continued sense of belonging to that cultural heritage, much of which she has essentially lost touch with while living in the United States.

Rita is a scrupulously honest person who likes to know where she stands with herself, other people, and the world. She has not become oppressed or a victim of her fairly harsh economic circumstances, because she knows that decisions she has made in her life, such as the one to emigrate to the United States, have had a strong impact on her life.

Although Rita has not had a successful career in conventional terms, she has maintained her self-respect through achieving her own economic independence and by parenting her children effectively. She has been married to the same man, who is also originally from Argentina, for 28 years and has a fairly calm, meaningful relationship with him. The trust she and her husband have for each other gives her additional strength and confidence. She counteracts some of the economic stringency and hardship of her living conditions by controlling how she spends her time and energy.

All of Rita's children have done well in their education and occupations. Three of her children are college educated, and two share in the ownership of small businesses. Rita is proud of their accomplishments. At the same time, she maintains respect for her own part in raising her children in her adopted country.

Hazel

Hazel is a white, middle-class accountant. She is a member of a large family that lives in the same city. Her mother and sisters are college educated, and all of them work outside the home.

Hazel has difficulty reconciling her career plans with her wish to have her own family. For a time, she considered marrying Bill, a banker. Bill is a fairly traditional man. She was afraid that he would be demanding about the timing of children and family size, and would expect that she should assume total responsibility for child care. After visiting Bill's family several times, Hazel decided against marrying Bill. She noticed that Bill's mother and sisters were consistently very subservient to the men in their family. She feared even more that this pattern would be repeated in her own marriage if she married Bill.

Hazel continued to date other men over a 10-year period, during which time she established herself professionally with a local firm of accountants. After she had been made a partner in the firm, she married Steve, a lawyer who had been divorced a few years before. Hazel knew that Steve's unhappy first marriage made him more willing to negotiate about roles and expectations for marriage. Because Steve did not have children from his first marriage, she felt that the remarriage circumstances were relatively simple, and that she would not be assuming many unusually complex or hidden responsibilities.

Throughout the lengthy period of career development and deliberation about marriage, Hazel stayed in close touch with her own family. Those contacts were empowering to her, because she took the opportunity to get to know herself better through increasing her family contacts, especially with relatives in her extended family. Over time, Hazel realized that her emotional security derives largely from her own family. As a result she does not burden her relationship with Steve unnecessarily with extraordinary claims for his attention to meet her needs. Steve shares responsibilities for caring for their two children, and both Hazel and Steve maintain close contact with their own families. Hazel continues to have a successful career and thrives within her marriage to Steve.

ANALYSIS AND INTERPRETATION

Faye, Rita, and Hazel are strengthened through their family connections. Although Faye does not have as large a family group as Rita and Hazel, she created an effective support network of friends and church groups in her neighborhood, as well as developing contact with relatives.

Stresses that Faye experiences as a single parent are relieved through her active participation in church groups, especially special interest groups such as the parenting group. Her identification with other young mothers means that she can effectively avoid some parenting problems before they arise. Learning from others becomes an effective tool for Faye in dealing with her routine daily pressures.

The reciprocal exchange of services that Faye developed helped to further connect her and her son to the community. She gained self-respect from being useful to others, and she continues to be a valued friend and neighbor. Her son continues to benefit from the variety of experiences that Faye makes possible for him through these exchanges.

Rita's contacts with her family span two continents and three generations. Although she had infrequent visits with her parents and older relatives since settling in the United States, she never closed the door to the possibility of returning to Argentina, especially in times of family need. The strength of roots in her family, in spite of her geographic distance from Argentina, gave her much stability and security in raising her own children.

Rita worked outside the home throughout the time that she parented. She alternated work hours with her husband and has been able to maintain some degree of economic independence throughout her marriage. Her forthright attitude makes her strong in dealing with her immediate family, as well as her older brothers. She has a no-nonsense approach that gains the respect of other people and helps her to get tasks accomplished with their cooperation.

Hazel fortunately learned from her mother and sisters how to achieve independence. Those women were strong models to learn from, and she was able to make wise decisions about her future based on these empowered women's examples in her own family. From an early age, Hazel knew some of the pitfalls to watch out for in planning marriage and children. Romance alone would not be sufficient to make her family life viable. She knew what she wanted in a working relationship with her spouse in her home, and she was not prepared to compromise.

This rich awareness and knowledge enabled Hazel to make a sensible choice in selecting Steve for her husband rather than Bill. She had learned from her mother and sisters that you cannot change your spouse's behavior and that she had better not organize her life around such a futile goal. The time and energy that Steve would willingly give her while they were raising their children would enable her to continue her professional career successfully, as well as give their children the benefits of having two loving and actively committed parents. Hazel knew that this quality of companionship in her marriage would be much more satisfying to her than the traditional division of labor situation that would have followed a decision to marry Bill.

CHOICES

In order to deal with their families—to transform their relationships with their families from those that are oppressive to those that lead to fulfillment—women need to understand the power of family influences on their lives. Women cannot attain this understanding without much effort. Making decisions is a vital and necessary preliminary to changing behavior so that it is clearly and constructively in women's own interests. First, they must choose to be open to the possibility that their actions are restricted by their families. Then they must choose to make changes in how they perceive themselves, other family members, and their respective responsibilities. Some of the critical choices related to family are enumerated below.

1   Women must choose to see themselves as members of many generations and as participants in complex emotional dependencies within their families. Unless they acknowledge the embeddedness and pervasiveness of these influences, they will not be able to change them.

2   As well as seeing the broader picture of their families, women must choose to examine the exchanges they make in the most significant two- and three-person relationships within their families. These units of analysis provide important facts about women's capacities for autonomous action in light of the intensity of key family influences.

3   Women must choose to see themselves and their own needs before meeting the needs of other family members. This choice of focus is essential. If women act only according to their conditioning, they will automatically put others before themselves in formulating their goals for everyday behavior.

4   Women must choose to have meaningful contacts with as many family members as possible. This relationship system is so significant that it influences the quality of all other social contacts. Unless women respond thoughtfully and deliberately to their families, they become pawns of the different social systems in which they participate.

5   Women must choose to maintain contact with their families, even though they also may choose to travel or lead careers that take them away from home. This contact will help them to stay centered in their lives, and generally will give them continuity and some security through time. A woman's cutting herself off from family contacts increases the probability of symptomatic behavior, just as staying exclusively within the family can restrict a woman's life.

6   The choice to change the traditional division of labor in families can free women sufficiently to avail themselves of the more diverse opportunities available in wider society. The real burdens women endure frequently derive from their families rather than from their work outside their homes.

GENERALIZATIONS

Some generalizations can be made about women's family roles, others' expectations for women in their families, and women's responsibilities for themselves and their families. Even if women never marry, they continue to be daughters, sisters, granddaughters, and nieces throughout their lives, and these roles have their own specific expectations and responsibilities.

Because families are the most significant emotional systems women and men participate in, family definitions have a strong impact on their lives. Women are expected to play the dominant roles in maintaining the well-being of all family members, without paying particular attention to their own well-being.

1 Women's family responsibilities must be coped with effectively in some way before women can function effectively in the wider society. However, women's status in their work outside the home can modify their positions in their families. As women gain more occupational responsibility, they are able to make more powerful decisions within their families.

2 Women can use their knowledge of family relationships to understand themselves more fully and to increase their emotional security. By establishing strong, autonomous positions within their families, women can function more effectively in other social groups.

3 It is particularly important for women to recognize the patterns of behavior and interdependence between grandmothers, mothers, sisters, and themselves. Women's networks within families, whether or not the networks are activated, establish emotional patterns of influence for crucial once-in-a-lifetime decisions, such as whether to marry, and at what age to marry. These patterns exert a defining impact on successive generations of women.

4 In order to understand the depth of women's conditioning, it is necessary for women to examine their family influences closely, especially those in the earliest years of their development. Family structure and demographics, such as spacing between siblings, and whether those siblings are female or male, have considerable influence on the way women are conditioned to see themselves and others.

5 In order to grow and empower themselves, women need to deal with the emotional issues that exist within their families. Tension around concerns, such as the division of labor for everyday chores or care of the elderly, must be dealt with effectively in order for women to be strong. If a resolution of these stresses does not occur, women's behavior will be less effective and possibly dysfunctional.

6 Women's hope for equity and the future derives from how the younger generation is raised. Transmitting egalitarian values to children is a vital task in the global objective of women's empowerment. Although women cannot accomplish this transmission of values without the cooperation of men, they must take the initiative to do it. It is usually not in men's interests to reduce their numerous privileges in a patriarchal society.

PROPOSITIONS

Some propositions can be made that specify women's choices more precisely, in light of the repetitions of behavior within families and between families and society. Although these correlations need much further substantiation, preliminary clinical data suggest that women can be empowered in the following ways.

1 The more closely connected to their families women remain, the more they will be able to function effectively in wider society. Women must not be rigidly tied to their families, but they benefit from not cutting themselves off from their families.

2 When women can effectively reformulate the traditional division of labor within the family, they are free to accomplish their goals in the wider society. Typically, it is not the work conditions outside their homes that burden women, but the need to accomplish their everyday tasks in their families.

3 The better women can understand themselves by examining the roles of other women in their families, the freer and more empowered they are. Women in their own families have a strong impact on defining younger women's role responsibilities. Women do not have an unimpeded view of society in their early socialization, because their families mediate society's values, and women generally internalize, at least initially, those values that their parents want them to have.

4 Women's understanding of themselves must include knowing the details of their early socialization. In addition to recognizing other women family members as role models, women need to know the kinds of emotionally significant events that occurred in their own earliest years, and how the gender dynamics of their families resolved those tensions.

5 The more egalitarian a family is, the more functional its members are. Clinical data suggest that an extreme polarization of gender roles within families is dysfunctional for all family members, as is a hierarchically organized family. Women function optimally when they are autonomous with respect to other family members.

6 Women grow *through* their families, not outside them. Their basic social needs require them to continue to interact with their families if they are to be empowered. Women need to change their traditional roles; but at the same time, in order to function most effectively, women must continue to interact with as many members of different generations as possible.

Chapter 6

Women and Religion

Historically, women have almost never held influential positions in the traditional organizational hierarchies of the major world religions (Christ 1983; van den Hoogen, 1990). In the lower ranks of religious organizations and in the more personal spheres of religious observance, women routinely outnumber men in adherence to devotional practices in both public and private settings. Within families, women frequently have a more significant impact than do their partners on the religious training and religious socialization of their children (Randour, 1987). Although women are not as visible as men in formal religious leadership, they are frequently more dominant in family religious activities (Shehan, Bock, & Lee, 1990).

Religion exerts a powerful controlling influence on most people's everyday beliefs. Religious values and beliefs tend to be conservative, which means that their influence may limit emotional and intellectual development (Berger & Luckmann, 1966; Weber, 1977). With respect to women, religion tends to sustain and even promote their social and economic subordination. The controlling and limiting influences of religion have particularly strong effects on women, because women are traditionally trained to be obedient and passive, as well as characteristically intense in their devotional practices (Caute, 1967; Daly, 1968).

Most established religions project a negative identity for women. Women are associated with sin and temptation and are perceived as threats to both patriarchal religion and society itself (Hays, 1964). This negativity has far-reaching social consequences; women are perceived as inferior beings, becoming relative outsiders of established social institutions (Christ, 1983; Durkheim, 1965).

Undoubtedly some women benefit from depending on religion and religious faith to support themselves through crises (Burdick, 1990; Hall, 1991). Although women may find it difficult to adhere to all the norms of a particular religion, they can develop their own inner faith in the context of and in response to the variety of existing denominations and sects (Luckmann, 1967). In fact, women's spiritual development is a source of great strength and empowerment for many different kinds of activities and changes (Christ & Plaskow, 1979; Randour, 1987). Religion and spirituality can be an effective basis for women's organization and unity.

The value orientations both women and men derive from religion frequently give them purpose and direction in their lives, whatever their ethnic or cultural settings may be (Kluckhohn & Strodtbeck, 1961; Weber, 1977). Furthermore, religion can be a means of guidance in dealing with practical matters such as family problems, even where a family has more than one religion, as in interfaith marriages (Shehan et al., 1990). In addition to functional practical orientations and problem-solving advantages, religion also can serve as a foundation for selection of values for women's new identities (Hammond, 1988). Who women believe they are is inextricably tied to their beliefs in natural and supernatural realities (Hall, 1990a).

As a result of many recent social changes, women are breaking patterns inherent in some of society's historical stereotyped expectations that they should be keepers of moral standards and models of moral virtue (Flowers, 1987). As other stereotypes linger, such as those that suggest that women can be demoniac or have inferior social values (Hays, 1974), women are discovering and demonstrating that they need to develop and strengthen their own values, as well as their own unique kinds of worship and spirituality (Haddad & Findler, 1985).

Feminists articulate new views about women's spiritual needs and their positions in relation to established patriarchal religions (Christ & Plaskow, 1979; Daly, 1973; Plaskow, 1983). It appears that it is timely to meet women's needs by acknowledging that religion and spirituality can serve as reliable and effective sources of empowerment (Hall, 1991). Religion is able to transform women's everyday attitudes and behavior in productive and constructive ways (Berger & Luckmann, 1966; Weber, 1977), rather than keep them in subordination as has been hypothesized previously (Caute, 1967). Religion is a means through which women's personal and unique experiences join broad social structures and history itself (Mills, 1967), having emboldening and empowering effects on their decisionmaking and behavior.

LIFE HISTORIES

In order to illustrate the empowering effects of religion on the lives of women, the religious lives of three women are described below. Some nuances of experiences of women who want to grow and change their lives included in the examples are sufficiently broad and far-reaching that they apply to other situations also.

Jennifer

Jennifer was raised as a Roman Catholic. She married a Protestant, but neither she nor her husband changed religions. Jennifer stayed committed to raising her two children as Roman Catholics. Although Jennifer could not share church-going activities with her husband, she regularly attended her own church alone and built up community contacts by frequenting a church close to her home.

Jennifer maintained a fairly large circle of friends from this church and frequently called her friends for advice and guidance. She and her friends helped each other in times of crisis, so this support was mutual and beneficial to all. Because her husband was not attentive or responsive, Jennifer found that it was imperative for her to live with a high level of emotional independence if she was to survive in her marriage. Her religious faith provided her with a frame of reference for her everyday thinking and decisionmaking, and the church was a place for her to socialize and take her children. Her husband was not a conventionally religious person, and this separation of their interests and activities was amicable. He spent time with "the boys" while she went to church.

After several years of reflecting about her preferred life-time goals and activities, Jennifer decided to change her part-time job to pursue a career as a pharmacist. She gained support and increased her optimism for this ambitious challenge from her church friends, and thus was able to withstand her husband's frequent criticism and sabotage during important early stages of the implementation of her plans for studies and career development.

In these and other respects, Jennifer's religion empowered her to pursue her own meaningful objectives in spite of her husband's resistance. Jennifer also was motivated to deal with her family responsibilities effectively through this support.

Mawi

Mawi is a Vietnamese immigrant who has suffered much abuse from her Vietnamese husband. She has two young children, and she is fearful that her husband will begin to hurt them. Although Mawi's ethnic religion is Buddhism, she has started to attend a local Protestant church. It is difficult for her to find a Buddhist place of worship near her home where she could continue her traditional devotions in a public setting.

Mawi's cultural background and lower social class membership make her particularly vulnerable to her husband's and boss's exploitation. She has an ill-paid job in a local laundry, and her husband does not share his laborer's pay fairly with her to meet the necessary household expenses. Mawi's Buddhist beliefs have oriented her to accept passively and readily whatever happens to her, but she is now forced to question how and whether she can continue to endure the pain of her husband's violence and his lack of economic support.

Over time, Mawi started to spend more time at her church. She participated in several self-help groups that were held there and were available to the community. She became good friends with some women participants, especially with those who understood her abusive family situation. Through the honesty and encouragement of these older and more experienced women, she learned that she had options and that she could get out of her dangerous situation.

Mawi's new religious beliefs strengthened her sense of self and her belief that there was a God who did not want her to go through life suffering as she did. Moved by the very real concern that the family violence would probably become worse rather than better, especially given her husband's pressured work situation, and the additional concern that she must act responsibly for her children's welfare as well as her own, Mawi decided to move out of her home. The church counselor directed Mawi to a women's shelter in another part of the city to enable her to make this transition effectively. The church also gave her some funds to make this difficult move.

When Mawi sought a new home in a different district, she chose one close to another church that had community activities. Although it was too dangerous for her to return to her former church and friends, she had discovered that church attendance and social contacts through the church gave her much needed support in these difficult times. Through help from the church community, Mawi has continued to function well and to support her children responsibly. She also found a better paying job for herself close to her new home.

Betty

Betty is a 60-year-old white woman who works in a bread factory. She has been widowed for 8 years. Her two daughters are raising their own young families in small towns in the western United States.

Betty has to work outside the home to support herself. However, her job is trying and dull, and she hopes that something will come her way that pays as well as her factory job and is at the same time more pleasant—especially because she is getting older.

Betty was raised as a Roman Catholic, but has been unable to attend her church since her husband's death. Whereas some people can find support in their traditional religion in times of crisis, Betty found herself utterly discouraged when her Roman Catholic religion and church attendance did not comfort her during her husband's illness. She first became disillusioned with the health care that her husband received in a Roman Catholic hospital, and then she found her church friends could not understand the agony she went through seeing her husband's pain during his long, drawn-out illness and death from cancer.

Betty is a self-educated woman who has always sought comfort and enjoyment from recreational reading. Because she is so geographically distant from her daughters and their families, she has to depend on her own resources for her daily sustenance and entertainment.

Betty discovered that some popular self-help books can help her to cope with her loneliness. She also watches televised evangelical services, and finds that her need to pray has persisted, although her formal worship at the Roman Catholic church has ceased. She cultivates a new daily schedule of prayer and meditation, being inspired by televised services and some of the religious pamphlets and books she purchases at a local bookstore.

Betty's ability to pray and meditate also protects her from boredom and some of the drudgery of her job. She uses prayer deliberately to fortify her attitude each day, and she finds that her health has improved considerably. Although her religious observances are not conventional, Betty empowers herself through strengthening specific religious beliefs. This effort helps her to transcend the limitations of the difficult situation in which she finds herself. The broader view of her life, which she gets from prayer and meditation, keeps her problems in perspective, and she is enabled to make the most of her possibilities.

ANALYSIS AND INTERPRETATION

These three examples show how religion, church attendance, and prayer can empower women. Although actual community contacts of church congregations are more palpable and reliable as supports, as they were for Jennifer and Mawi, prayer and meditation outside the context of church attendance, as in the case of Betty, can also be supportive and inspiring.

Jennifer's experience showed how maintaining her own religion fortified her in her interfaith marriage, especially in the particular situation of having a strained relationship with her husband. Jennifer was able to find meaning through her church attendance, as well as to revitalize her rather empty life through the church activities she attended. After a few months of this support, she became able to motivate herself to make a satisfying career plan.

Mawi's church attendance became a life-saving resource for her and her two children. Although she had not realized that she was in a life-threatening situation when she first started to attend the Protestant services close to her home, the love and support she received through the church made her realize that following the advice to leave her husband was in her own interest and especially in the interest of her children.

It can be surmised that Mawi's original Buddhist upbringing predisposed her to be victimized by her husband. However, Mawi's ability to turn this attitude around to one that is courageous shows that religion does not necessarily impede women's independence. The individualistic emphasis of Protestantism had some appeal for Mawi in her plight of needing to adapt to the values of the United States in order to survive.

Betty essentially changed her religion during her husband's fatal illness. Although she did not formally convert to another religion, she clearly turned her back on Roman Catholicism and embraced a more fundamentalist version of Protestantism. Betty's loneliness and alienation at work made her particularly vulnerable to sectarian beliefs and self-help formulae. To the extent that Betty read about religion and thought about it seriously, however, these changes improved her life. Her newfound faith allowed her to be more optimistic and to see opportunities for improving her life in everyday situations. Betty's prayer and meditation fortified her rather than debilitated her in her difficult living situation.

CHOICES

These three life histories illustrate some of the choices women make to answer innate concerns about the ultimate nature of their existence. The ways in which women conceptualize and experience God or a supreme being influence the quality of their everyday existence.

1 Women must deliberately choose their religious beliefs rather than accept them blindly, whatever the denominational or sectarian source of those beliefs.

2 Women must choose the degree of intensity with which they affiliate to a religion. The degree of religiosity they have determines the ways in which beliefs founded in religion are manifested in their daily behavior.

3 Women's beliefs in God or a supreme being imply specific choices in their understanding of human nature. Depending on how much power women attribute to God, and consequently to themselves, they will think of themselves and behave as though they are either independent or pawns of fate.

4 Even if women have no particular religious affiliation, they must make some choices about the nature of ultimate reality in order to function effec-

tively. Women's choices in resolving such universal concerns orient them to the world, to other people, and to themselves.

5 World religions are patriarchal. Women define the ways they perceive gender and equality through their choices of religion. Unless women are convinced that all people are equal in the eyes of God, they will believe that they are inferior.

6 Women can choose to maintain ties to traditional religious beliefs and at the same time achieve autonomy, equality, and independence. This balance is not easily won, however, because women have to make a conscious effort in order to maintain their own throughout their religious participation.

GENERALIZATIONS

An examination of the patterns in religious participation and the quality of women's lives shows that historically and across cultural boundaries religion has tended to reinforce women's subordination in society. This limitation on women deprives them of a dependable source of motivation to lead their lives responsibly as independent moral agents.

Some of the common characteristics about religion that affect women's choices and their level of collective action in society are listed below. Religion need not limit women's behavior, although the restrictive influences of a religion inevitably impinge upon women's freedom.

1 Religious socialization trains women to be single-minded in their devotion to family responsibilities. Most religions present other work options for women in a less advantageous light.

2 Traditional religions sanctify male values—through the personification of God as "He," male leadership in formal religious organizations, and the content of religious belief systems. Female values, except those that produce and support women's subordination, are not significant in world religions.

3 Religious beliefs foster a strong passive orientation to life in women. Women are indoctrinated to be obedient through their religious training and devotional practices. A "good" woman is a traditional woman, and this definition and associated expectations are strengthened through moral sanctions.

4 Religion views women's traditional behavior as part of a sacred and natural order that should be maintained and revered. Women's questioning of the status quo and their actions to increase egalitarianism are perceived as being suspect or even diabolical.

5 Women's empowerment may include their incorporation of strong religious beliefs and motives in their everyday behavior. Reflection and contemplation enable women to find religious rationales in denominational and sectarian religions for their free and liberating behavior. Independent women should not be deprived of traditional religious affiliations. They can benefit from cultivating their relationships with a supreme being through prayer, meditation, and ritualistic observance.

6 Women need vision in these times of rapid social change. Religion is a valuable source of values and ideals, and closeness with some religious traditions can fortify women for the necessarily difficult effort to obtain equity.

PROPOSITIONS

Generalizations can be further refined to suggest correlations and explanations that need substantiation through life history and research data. The propositions given below relate to ways in which religion can inhibit women's lives and ways in which religion can liberate women—that is, enable women to live out a destiny of being equal in the eyes of God.

Although religion tends to reinforce social class differences as well as gender differences in activities and accomplishments, religion is also a source of values that is available to all. Religious values are usually guarded by male elites, but direct communion with a supreme being can unite women with these strong motivating ideals.

1   The more deliberate women are in choosing religious beliefs, the more capable they will be of building their autonomy in connection with established religious traditions. Autonomy that derives from traditional religion is stronger and more secure than an artificially contrived independence.

2   The more women can satisfactorily answer their own questions about the nature of ultimate reality, the more effective women will be in their everyday behavior. Women's breadth of vision will enhance the quality of their negotiations with others.

3   Religion is one of the most meaningful contexts in which women can evaluate their vocations. Women's work needs to be seen in the broadest perspective possible in order for women to be able to fully evaluate it, and religious dimensions give this evaluation breadth.

4   To the extent that women do not question their religious beliefs, they run a correspondingly greater risk of being further subordinated. Male interests are predominant in established religions. Women must be aware of this patriarchal domination before they can benefit from achieving equal access to religious inspiration.

5   A model of worship for women as partners of a supreme being frees women to fill their human divine potentials through everyday behavior. When women realize they not only need God but that God needs them as well, they will become increasingly autonomous.

6   Increased religious participation gives women a sense of community in an anonymous society. Also, established religions organize groups to meet specific educational and family needs. Women empower themselves when they break through their isolation by exchanging ideas and experiences with other women in these settings.

Chapter 7

Women and Work

It has only been in the last 20 years that a large proportion of women have worked outside the home fairly consistently throughout their working lives (Feinstein, 1979). In lower social classes, women traditionally have worked outside the home by necessity, hoping to become sufficiently well-off someday to stay at home and care for their families (Bott, 1957; Gerson, 1985). Due to recession and the inflated cost of living, increasing numbers of women from all social classes in the United States are working outside of the home by necessity. The dual-earner family continues to become more typical throughout the population than the middle-class nuclear family, in which generally only husbands and fathers work outside the home (Aldous, 1982; Hood, 1983; Pleck, 1985).

For the first time, empirical data are being used to document some of the kinds of links between women's work outside the home and their work at home. Recent research findings substantiate the observation that women not only suffer discrimination on the job (Portocarero, 1989); frequently, they are also limited in their decisionmaking powers in the home. It is only when women have considerable autonomy and decisionmaking authority at their workplace outside the home that this tends to be correlated with increased autonomy and decisionmaking power at home (Blau, 1967; Ross, 1987). Generally speaking, we can summarize the complexities and nuances in these trends by stating that most women are limited by a traditional division of labor both at home and in the workforce (Aytac, 1990; Durkheim, 1984; Reskin & Hartman, 1986).

Although women's criteria for social class distinctions differ from men's criteria of social classes (Caute, 1967; Charles, 1990), in reality men's social class definitions have more influence in society at large, and women's opportunities are largely restricted by the economic standing of their husbands or fathers (Davis, 1983; Wilson, 1980). Women's work, which could be a basis of their own social class placement, is frequently confined to nonpaying or underpaying jobs inside and outside the home (Bergmann, 1981; Howe, 1977; Oakley, 1975, 1976).

When women manage to rise out of their subordinated social and economic positions by doing work that has more status and pay, they find that they are discriminated against in token positions of advancement (Kauppinen, Haavio-Mannila, & Kandolin, 1989) and among women's and men's elites (Baxter & Lansing, 1983). As a result of the pervasiveness of these pressures at work, most women are unable to move from their economic subordination and subjugation (Beauvoir, 1974; Chodorow, 1978). Those women who manage to develop their work skills and pursue career directions frequently do not have the resources to assist other women to break out of their occupational limitations (Aga, 1984).

Women's traditional functions in society and their value orientations limit their views of themselves and the world (Bernard, 1981; Weber, 1977). Crises such as divorce bring severe economic hardship and the burdensome necessity to work outside the home regardless of preference, especially when women have children (Weitzman, 1985). The monotonous work that these women are often obliged to undertake relentlessly narrows their lives and impoverishes them (Pearce, 1983; Westwood, 1985).

In some respects, only broad economic changes will enable women to be paid according to the value of the goods and services they produce (Engels, 1970; Kahn-Hut, Daniels, & Colvard, 1982; Steinberg & Haignere, 1984). To accomplish this, capitalism would have to be more radically modified than vested interests would readily permit (Eisenstein, 1979), although women's individual and collective well-being depends on changes in established economic structures.

Women who work outside of the home increasingly establish their identities based on their occupations. In this respect, work choices outside the home are becoming increasingly central concerns in women's expressions of their values and their personal and professional fulfillment. Although women may not be motivated to work outside the home solely for the purpose of social class mobility, as many men appear to be (Charles, 1990), they increasingly find meaning through their work accomplishments (Weber, 1977).

LIFE HISTORIES

The three life histories below illustrate the interplay between limiting economic conditions in women's lives, and women's transcendence of these impediments through their choices and accomplishments. Women generally still have an inordinately disproportionate share of family responsibilities, which they must necessarily balance with their outside work needs and demands. However, life history data show that they can become freer at home—through a more egalitarian sharing of domestic chores and parenting, and through paying for housekeeping and maintenance services—when they gain decisionmaking responsibilities and autonomy in their work outside the home.

Veronica

Veronica is a white, lower-class, single parent who has two young children to support. She receives no financial assistance from her children's father.

Veronica tried to earn her living through secretarial work, but the rigors of a regular office job and its low pay forced her to try other options. However, after experimenting with being a waitress and a shop assistant, Veronica decided to get training in computer skills in order to be eligible for more adequate pay in an office setting.

Veronica's progress in learning these new skills was slow. She did not receive any substantial pay raises until she had advanced beyond elementary computer skills. By accepting only temporary office work, Veronica retained sufficient autonomy to manage her complicated schedule and demanding family responsibilities. When her children were sick, she took her work home.

In time, through on-the-job training, Veronica acquired more advanced computer and management skills, and she moved into a part-time administrative position. Her persistence in acquiring practical business knowledge and her new career direction paid off by making her further advancement possible.

Veronica continued to place a high priority on earning an adequate living and having a career. After both of her children started public school, she took a full-time position in a local government department. She continued to work on her professional development very successfully. She gained much self-confidence and pride through her accomplishments.

Lara

Lara is a middle-aged Puerto Rican woman. Out of necessity, Lara must work to supplement her husband's income, because she and her husband are paying for their two children to go to college.

At one time, Lara and her husband worked for the same shoe company, although Lara received considerably lower wages for performing less-skilled, routine tasks than her husband did for performing more specialized labor. Lara did not enjoy the work she did. She found it boring, stressful, and unrewarding. Lara's children commute to a local college, so they were still able to help with some of the household chores, but Lara's husband did not assist her in organizing their domestic lives. Lara felt trapped by her home and factory responsibilities.

When Lara realized that she might have an unnecessarily stressful daily routine, she began to talk to friends about how she could create a more meaningful life for herself. She decided to attend classes to improve her skills in reading and writing English, so that she could eventually find better work.

After several months, Lara left her factory job for a joint venture—a beauty shop—with a woman friend who is also Puerto Rican. Lara's friend has considerable business experience and language facility, and Lara is able to depend on her friend for the necessary administration of the shop. At the same time, Lara is using the opportunity to acquire new skills.

Although Lara's family has not reduced their demands on her energies at home, they now give her considerably more respect for making the change in her work life. At the outset of her new business venture, Lara could not contribute as much income to her children's education as she had been giving previously; they had to work to support themselves. Now that a few months have passed, however, Lara has begun to bring home as much money as she had done before. At the same time, she is substantially more satisfied by working in her own business venture.

Rachel

Rachel is a white, middle-class lawyer. She has a high income and has decided to further her career rather than marry and have children.

At one time, Rachel lived with Joe, a university professor. Joe did much of his professional work at home and took care of many of the domestic chores while Rachel worked outside of the home. Joe had been married previously. He and his former wife had three children who now live with their mother. Joe had decided not to remarry and not to have more children, so he and Rachel were fairly compatible.

Sometimes, Joe did pressure Rachel to spend more time at home, and Rachel felt guilty about not wanting to be with him. However, her discomfort was only fleeting because she had worked very hard to reach her position in her law firm. She knew that she needed to handle overtime tasks and unexpected client requests in order to be in a good position to compete for more professional advancement.

After a year of conflict over what Joe characterized as Rachel's lack of responsiveness to his requests and eventual demands that she be at home in the evenings, Rachel decided to move out of the apartment and find a place of her own. She was disappointed that her romance and friendship with Joe had not worked out, but her life priorities were to pursue her career as wholeheartedly as she could.

Two years later, Rachel was made a partner in her law firm. She also formed a new relationship with David, a colleague she saw frequently at professional meetings. She and David lived in different cities, where each had their own apartment. Shortly after being promoted, Rachel and David decided to live together.

Rachel and David have kept their two apartments in different cities. Each pays for housekeeping and maintenance assistance to take care of domestic chores in his or her apartment. Although neither Rachel nor David enjoys the complexities of their commuter relationship, Rachel is much happier with a less emotionally involved commitment than she would be if she had a possessive, needy husband or lover sharing her home in the same city. She knows that she cannot conform to the conventions of a middle-class marriage, and this is a satisfying compromise for her.

ANALYSIS AND INTERPRETATION

Veronica, Lara, and Rachel each made decisions that empowered them through improving their work situations. Although Rachel, who has the most economic success, is clearly the one who has gained the most autonomy at home, both Veronica and Lara have been able to increase their independence as well. Veronica has made a series of decisions that continue to enable her to advance professionally. Lara changed the conditions of her work outside the home so that her family deals with her in more cooperative and respectful ways.

Veronica is an unusually resourceful person. Considering her continuing burden of child-care responsibilities and her one-time inadequate work skills, her achievements are impressive. She persisted in her efforts to better her position, in spite of realistically low odds for succeeding. She believed and continues to believe in herself sufficiently to allow her to experiment in a variety of work activities. As a result of this risk-taking spirit, she is able to decide fairly easily about what she thinks is best for her and for her particular situation.

Veronica is skillful in handling computer and management training together with meeting her children's needs. In spite of her relative ambition, she chose to have a part-time job until the children were in public school. The strength and fortitude she had in this situation paid off later through her rapid advancement when she started to work full-time in the government position.

Lara is a creative person who felt deadened by her routine work in the shoe factory. Although she knew she could not count on her husband for emotional support in her work decisions, she nevertheless decided to make major changes by joining her friend in a business. Lara's willingness to study English and business skills means that this change is not superficial for her or her family.

She has become a more powerful role model to her college student children, and she no longer accepts the conventional dominance of her working-class husband. She has gained a great deal of emotional support, as well as work satisfaction, by being in business with her friend.

Rachel was already an empowered woman. She had made many important career decisions in order to become a lawyer. Because of the effort she had invested in her profession, and because of her decision not to marry and have children, she was not willing to put up with a relationship with someone like Joe, who pressured her to do something she had decided not to do at this stage of her life. She would not allow Joe to blackmail her emotionally, especially because they did not have a marriage commitment or a family together.

Rachel's ability to wait until a more mature relationship could be built into her personal life worked out well for her. She was prepared to go through the inconveniences of commuting in order to be with someone who understood her professional interests and ambitions. She organized her household wisely by paying for as much help as she needed in her home. This decision also empowered her, by leaving her sufficient time and energy to do what she really wanted to do.

CHOICES

Although many women do not have a sufficiently full range of work options, there are some choices that are critical in women's decisions to work both inside and outside the home. Sometimes women's refusal to take on specific work responsibilities can be a more effective influence than their agreement to conform to others' expectations.

Some of the choices women have in relation to their work are listed here. Even women's attitudinal changes about their work can have distinct behavioral and social consequences. Women have the right to choose which choices they will make with regard to the services they will perform for others.

1 Women can choose the arena for their work. Traditional male values imply that a woman should work only in a family. Once women stretch their thinking to consider ways in which they can make contributions to communities and society, they find that their roles and behavior will change dramatically.

2 Women can choose which of their diverse activities will be of most importance to them. By deliberately establishing their priorities, women can broaden their perspectives and balance their lives more comfortably.

3 Women can choose which work to do based on their own skills and interests, as well as others' expectations. When women heighten their sense of self, they are more likely to choose those occupations that they truly prefer, even when they must work out of economic necessity.

4 Women's choice to be paid for the work they do is a critical step toward gaining economic independence. Economic independence is an essential base of

autonomy, and women will have more power in their domestic spheres when they can achieve some degree of status and recognition in their occupations.

5 Choosing their hours to work gives women some control over their work lives. Having either part- or full-time work outside of their homes does not mean that women must accept domestic responsibilities. Although house-keeping standards may suffer, delegating chores to others—or leaving tasks undone—can bring some relief to these pressures.

6 Women can choose to give an example of independence to their children through their work responsibilities. It is not as important that women earn large amounts of money—even though they deserve to receive good wages—as that they maintain some control over their lives and develop their real interests.

GENERALIZATIONS

When women are aware of some of the patterns that exist in their work activities, they will be more able to protect themselves from others' exploitations and to express themselves meaningfully through their work. Distinctions must be made between the paid and unpaid work that women do, and between the work they do out of and in the home.

1 Women tend to assume most of the domestic responsibilities for house-work and child care. Even when women work outside the home, they tend to continue to assume the same proportion of those responsibilities.

2 When women have sufficiently high incomes through their work outside the home, they are able to afford to employ domestic help and have other paid maintenance services. This relieves some women of much of the hard labor they would do in their homes, but usually they keep heavy supervisory respon-sibilities because they are familiar with the work that needs to be done by the employed help.

3 Equality may be achieved more easily in work settings outside the home than in the home. Women's mobility on the job is frequently more restricted by their domestic burdens than by discrimination from the work system.

4 Women's views of their work possibilities are limited by others' expec-tations and by tradition. Only when women can see themselves assuming career development paths effectively will they be able to pursue lines of work in their own real interests.

5 Religion can be a source of motivation for women's vocations, both inside and outside of the home. Values and beliefs lend considerable meaning to women's work orientations, and this support is a powerful resource that can assist women in their search for equity.

6 A life time plan for work is reasonable for all women, whatever their social class or ethnic group. Although many working-class women aspire to a life of domestic responsibilities rather than work outside the home, realistically women cannot be independent unless they have some reliable means of securing income.

PROPOSITIONS

Propositions suggest predictabilities and correlations in women's work activities. Although these factors derive from generalizations that may be made about women's work lives, they are more specific in their implications.

1 The more control women have over their time and energy when they work outside the home, the more able they will be to control their own participation in the domestic sphere.

2 In order to counteract their tendency to assume domestic responsibilities as well as responsibilities for work outside the home, women must be deliberately selective and eliminate as many unnecessary activities as possible. The more consciously women act with regard to their work decisions, the freer they will be to use their energies for activities that mean the most to them.

3 The more women are able to plan careers for themselves, the more likely they are to accomplish those plans. In order to concentrate on career planning, women need to see that their independence is tied to the paid work they can do.

4 To the extent that women can pay for work to be done in their homes, they will be freer to develop occupational goals in their own interests. Women must avoid being overburdened with domestic chores, as they are the only ones who will care enough about their survival and fulfillment in more meaningful activities.

5 When women see the connections between their work and their social class standing, they will be more empowered to make decisions that run counter to others' expectations. Social class definitions are largely male hierarchical categories, and women need not conform to these aspects of patriarchal authority.

6 Although economic independence is essential for women, the degree of satisfaction they receive from their work is also vital. Women will be motivated to make changes in society when they feel fulfilled by their work activities. For this reason it is important for women to focus on the meaningfulness of their work, as well as on the remuneration they receive.

Chapter 8

Women in the World

History makes us aware of the many different patterns in women's culture through time and space (Aries, 1965; Beard, 1971; Beauvoir, 1974; Chafetz & Dworkin, 1986; Evans, 1977). When contemporary women know more about different historical and cultural groups of women, they are able to understand themselves more fully, as well as to see the limitations and opportunities of their own lives more clearly (Shibutani, 1955). Having knowledge of women in different parts of the world makes it more possible to delineate the influence of women's and men's values on social change (Weber, 1977), and to see how societies have tended to undervalue women, whatever their historical circumstances, social standing, or cultural conditions (Schur, 1984).

The experiences of different ethnic groups in the United States also help us to see the almost infinite variety of women's activities throughout the world (Frazier, 1939; Glick, 1985; Staples, 1973). Whether class differences are becoming more influential than biological ethnic distinctions (Wilson, 1980) or cultural ethnic heritage (Gerth & Mills, 1946) in defining the wide variety of women's circumstances is perhaps not as important in determining the range of their experiences as is the strength of the bonds between women within the ethnic groups (Hill, 1972). It is only women's awareness of each other that can lead to more concerted efforts to accomplish local, national, and international changes.

In examining research about women throughout the world, we discover that there are some common denominators of experiences, particularly with respect to women's sexual and procreative functions and the division of labor at home and in society (Durkheim, 1984). In contemporary, highly industrialized societies, women have more choices to make about their own values, lives (Hall, 1990a, 1990b), and basic sexual and procreative functions (Bowen, 1978). The ways in which women see themselves are also influenced by their particular cultural contexts (Intons-Peterson, 1988) and their ages (Larsson & Olson, 1988).

One of the constants women have to achieve and adapt to is how to relate to men, particularly those men who are emotionally closest to them (Haas, 1981). The political systems of nation-states modify the relationships between women and men, especially where modern welfare states have replaced traditional societies (Dencik, 1989). We do not always quickly see the relationship between our daily lives and the power wielded by governments (Mills, 1967), but each woman's life history is inextricably bound to the political and economic conditions of the society in which she lives (Berteaux, 1981; Caute, 1967; Charlton, Everett, & Staudt, 1989).

One of the "ready-made" answers to the need for international social reorganization to achieve more equity between women and men is the development and adoption of socialism. Welfare societies in Europe, for example, exist most frequently in socialist countries or regimes (Caute, 1967; Flanz, 1983; Heckscher, 1984). Some attempts have been made to assess directly the effectiveness of socialism in meeting women's needs (Holter, 1984) and examine women's access to power in different countries (Epstein & Coser, 1981), as well as women as a social and economic class across national boundaries (Charles, 1990; Davis, 1983). The most radical documentation and interpretation of existing inequalities between women and men suggest militant theses that call for revolution (Firestone, 1971).

Where socialist countries have developed strong welfare states, as in Scandinavia, patriarchal structures and processes have been documented as coexisting with economic and legal reforms (Holter, 1984). Furthermore, in these same welfare states, some women have become overly dependent on state support for their own subsistence, especially at critical life stages such as childbirth or old age (Waerness & Ringen, 1987).

During the last two decades, a few selected middle- and upper-class women have been able to move from being subordinated to tradition to having token participation in political elites (Baxter & Lansing, 1983; Garcia de Leon, 1990). However, even in the most highly industrialized countries, a fairly consistent gap remains between the political and economic power held by women and men. In many respects, when compared to conditions in less-developed countries, and conditions prior to attempts at change, there is no significant reduction in the power differential between women and men in highly developed economies (Iglitzin & Ross, 1986). In contemporary Japan, for example, the lives of the large majority of women remain highly restricted and tradition-bound (Condon, 1985).

When women break into public life, they must necessarily let go of some of their traditional "inwardness" (Bernard, 1971; Robins-Mowry, 1983). Occupational mobility is an acceptable and effective means to increase women's freedom (Morgan, 1982; Portocarero, 1989), and women's occupational and professional subcultures become valued by the rest of society (Rosaldo & Lamphere, 1974).

Many women in different cultural settings move away from traditional family responsibilities (Trost, 1984) by being motivated by the ideal of equality (Stetson, 1987) or the right to be human (Scott, 1982). Other women seek religious or spiritual motivation, rather than ideological rationales. The major world religions, however, generally resist women's changes in their functions and status, thereby slowing the pace of increase of women's equity (Haddad & Findly, 1985). In spite of the resistance of religion and the limited appeal of ideological women's movements, the very existence of a social movement of international feminism (Duchen, 1987) suggests that women everywhere are beginning to create new identities for themselves and to increase their equity and equality (Diaz-Diocaretz & Zavala, 1985).

LIFE HISTORIES

The three examples given below illustrate the influence of international conditions on women and highlight the fact that women's empowerment is not being achieved in social, cultural, and economic vacuums. The experiences and opportunities of women in different parts of the world have a direct impact on the lives of women in other countries, regardless of whether an individual country's population of women is conscious of that influence. Although economic criteria and cultural conditions may not be the ultimate determing influences in women's lives, it is clear that women can be thought of as a social class or social institution within society. The repeated finding of social data documenting women's subservience and their sexual or procreative functions in most societies shows that women's passivity and their activities are used to maintain patriarchies in many crucial ways.

Min

Min is a Japanese American who received university-level education in France as well as in the United States. In spite of her intellectual sophistication as a linguist, and her varied cultural experience, she maintains strictly traditional

Japanese family loyalties and expectations. She plans to marry and have two children before she is 30 years old, and to abandon her career for parenting and domestic responsibilities. She is more than willing to be introduced to young men of her parents' choosing in order to select an appropriate husband, and she appears to exert very little independent influence on this process.

Min insists that she has made these choices freely—even though her preferences reflect the strong wishes of her parents. Min sees what she is doing in a broad context. She does not think of herself as a victim of circumstances, and she says she does not act in this way merely to please her parents and brothers.

Min's parents' wealth enables her to visit Europe, as well as Japan. This geographical separation gives her additional time for reflection, and her visits abroad reinforce her views. She continues to accept traditional Japanese ways of selecting a husband and believes that this decision is in her best long-term interest.

Ingrid

Ingrid is a naturalized American who was born and raised in Sweden. She worked as a commercial artist in a large city in the United States almost all of her adult life. She is unmarried and is now a senior citizen. Ingrid has been fiercely independent throughout her many intense friendships with women and men through the years. Now that she is older, she continues to thrive from the nurturing of her network of friends.

When Ingrid was younger, she did not value marriage or children. Moreover, after coming to the United States, she compared life in the United States with life in Sweden. She realized that there were so few family support programs in the United States, that family life would be much more difficult in the United States than in Sweden. Also, she found that single life was much more accepted and more usual among middle classes in Sweden than in the United States. Her awareness of the need for family support programs and her own reluctance to make a commitment to marry and have children made her even more independent in the United States than she would have been in Sweden.

Ingrid's early upbringing in Sweden also allowed her to become friends with men more easily than do women raised in the United States. She has a strong sense of equality and equity and has established several long-standing, open friendships with both women and men.

Now that she is a senior citizen, Ingrid plans to live with some of her old friends. She pursues her interests in art by setting up a daily routine whereby she can work effectively at home.

Ingrid returns to Sweden fairly frequently to visit with her younger relatives. Although she does not make this journey as often as she did when her parents and sister were alive, she still values this contact with her homeland and finds that her visits give her a new perspective on her life in the United States. She also finds that her health improves when she makes these visits.

Jacqueline

Jacqueline is a middle-aged, middle-class, French woman who married an American 20 years ago, came to the United States, and raised two children. She did not complete her college education and regrets that she has not had a career. Her conventional ways and her insistence on a graceful life-style determined that her energies were used in other ways.

Jacqueline is very invested in the future welfare of her daughter and son. She wants both of them to have opportunities and careers, unlike herself. In order to support these plans, Jacqueline started to work part-time in a local French restaurant. Her pay supplements her husband's income, which makes it possible for them to meet the high costs of their children's college education.

In some respects, Jacqueline's work is fulfilling. Her work takes her out of the home, and her new friends at work think she is charming and intelligent. Her world has been opened up considerably through her contacts at the restaurant, and the social stimulation she gets in her work makes her feel more alive, with more possibilities for her own life. She wants to increase her work hours to full-time and to develop a career in the restaurant business.

Having some independent income also changed other aspects of Jacqueline's isolation. Although her resources were very limited, because she was earning money she felt more able to travel to France and visit her family. She became somewhat estranged from her parents through her marriage to an American, but with her newfound independence she felt ready to reestablish meaningful contact with them, as well as to rediscover her French heritage.

While Jacqueline was in France, she was able to realize more easily that her cultural conditioning to be a passive, conventional married woman was very strong. Although she did not yet feel able to make many independent moves in her life in the United States, she returned to her adopted home with more awareness of the limitations that had trapped her in a narrowly restricted domestic mold throughout her marriage. She knew that life in France would have been equally circumscribed, if not more so, but she had not fully realized these restrictions until she had returned to France to visit her family.

ANALYSIS AND INTERPRETATION

The lives of the women in these examples illustrate how cultural influences modify women's expectations of themselves. Although Japan, Sweden, and France are all industrialized countries, there are marked contrasts, as well as similarities, in the degrees of independence customarily allowed to women in those settings.

Min, Ingrid, and Jacqueline are all traditional women in that their cultural heritages have a distinct impact on their values and behavior. Whereas Min and Jacqueline were originally from hierarchical societies (Japan and France, respectively), and were influenced by those values, Ingrid was strongly influenced by the more egalitarian values of Sweden.

Although Min appears to have been deferring to her parents' wishes, it is more accurate to say that she decided to conform to her parents' expectations and traditional Japanese customs. Min is well-educated, well-traveled, and sophisticated. She is not indecisive about her preferences with respect to marriage and career, and even later travel did not make her doubt the wisdom of her decision.

Min is empowered by her resolution to go in a specific direction in her life. Although at present she does not contemplate any need to revise her view, the fact that she is proceeding in a particular direction with deliberation means that she is more able to plan her future life and stay reasonably in control of her circumstances. In spite of deliberately restricting her world to the domestic sphere, she will undertake these responsibilities creatively and with enjoyment, rather than out of a sense of empty duty.

Ingrid is the most independent of the three women described. She not only pursued her interest in art throughout her successful work life, but continues to do so in her retirement. Her independent life-style is conducive to supporting her artistic talents and temperament. Ingrid is also empowered by the support of a sufficient number of good women and men friends. She is not an emotionally dependent person, and she maintains satisfying long-term bonds with them. Ingrid's visits to Sweden inspire her to maintain her Swedish cultural heritage in her life in the United States. Her Swedish respect for independence and equality has served her well in the less open cultural setting of the United States. In addition, her Swedish background encourages her to be quite comfortable with her single status.

The scope of Jacqueline's life continues to be fairly limited, but she has at least caught a glimpse of a more independent life-style that is possible because she has more independent economic means. Now that she has tasted these new freedoms, she will not be able to return easily to her former, more restricted status.

Although Jacqueline started her restaurant job to pay for her children's education, many of the benefits from widening the circle of her contacts accrue to her directly. Although she continues to pay part of her children's expenses, she now works more for her own needs than for their needs. Her recent consideration of full-time work and her openness to career possibilities further empower her.

Jacqueline's visit to France healed her estrangement from her parents. She deepened her understanding of herself through her contacts with her parents, and she gained a much-needed perspective on her life in the United States by being in France. An awareness of French culture makes Jacqueline more aware of the influence of French values on her behavior. The fact that she is interested in continuing to work in a restaurant with French cuisine and atmosphere means that she will gain greater continuity and further benefits from the deepening of her experience of her cultural heritage.

CHOICES

Women's perceptions of themselves and the world result from the choices they make. Their understanding flows from the values they cherish most, as well as from the facts of the situations in which they find themselves. Facts and values about women in the world at large can change women's perceptions of themselves and others.

When women know more about the choices other women have made in varied cultural and historical settings, they are in a stronger position to evaluate the choices that they must make. As the factual bases of women's lives expand, their judgments become more objective and more responsive to their own best interests. Increased options for women derive, in part, from the choices listed below.

1 Women can choose to educate themselves about women in different cultural and historical settings. Whether they are aware of the benefits of this effort or not, the new knowledge eventually will increase their wisdom and strength, making them more able to deal with their experiences.

2 Women choose to be open to possibilities for change when they are willing to see the world differently through their knowledge of the experiences of other women. By identifying with women in different countries, women can begin to see some of the universal dimensions of their lives.

3 Women will be able to understand diverse ethnic groups more fully when they choose to become informed about the influence of contrasting cultural values on women's options. Optimally, this fuller understanding will unify women; at least it will lead them to more concerted efforts to achieve collective goals.

4 Women's actions in the world at large show the range of possibilities for women's functioning in varied patriarchal societies. Although existing conditions do not determine women's potential, choosing to know these facts is a useful starting point for accomplishing the kinds of changes that are central to women's interests.

5 When women choose to see themselves in a world context, that broader perspective makes them more objective. Objectivity enhances women's reflections about their responsibilities to themselves and others.

6 Women can more satisfactorily understand the impact of cultural influences on the whole of their life course when they choose to compare and contrast their own experiences with the experiences of women in different societies. They can anticipate pressures on them when they know how other women are treated in varied historical and cultural settings.

GENERALIZATIONS

Patterns in women's work lives are repeated in different social contexts. Although there are marked contrasts in the experiences of women in different classes, ethnic groups, and cultures, there are also similarities in their roles as subordinates.

One challenge of change is to rise above the predictabilities of generalizations. Women are not determined by statistical trends, but knowing what these trends are increases their freedom—they know what pressures and odds they are up against in carving out their own courses. The generalizations below suggest directions for change.

1 As almost all societies are patriarchal, women's subordination is essentially universal. This does not mean that women's subordination will necessarily continue in perpetuity, but it does suggest that it will be inordinately difficult to make changes that accomplish egalitarian relations.

2 All women work. For some work, they are paid; for some work, they are not paid. Work that is in the home or on the family property, especially in agricultural settings, is usually not done for pay. The dichotomy between women's work in the home and their work outside the home might be more accurately stated in terms of distinguishing between work for which pay is and is not received.

3 A fairly constant trend throughout modern industrialized countries is that when women work outside the home, they also are expected to continue their traditional responsibilities of domestic work and parenting. When women do not get promoted on the job, it is due as much, if not more, to their having heavy domestic responsibilities as to the presence of discrimination against them at their places of work.

4 Women who achieve the highest status in their work outside the home are frequently those who do not marry, or those who have only a few children. This suggests that worldwide it is women who live up to male norms who perform with the highest degree of social recognition for their efforts.

5 In modern industrialized countries, women live longer than do men in the same social class or ethnic group. Men, as active risktakers, may shorten their lives by stresses they invite; women may know more about balance and wisdom in dealing with their everyday demands, thereby lengthening their lifespan.

6 In a world context, both families and religion reinforce women's economic subordination. Women's empowerment can level these influences so that more egalitarian relations come into being.

PROPOSITIONS

Propositions about women in the world can become bases for strategies to free women from their subordination. Propositions imply predictability, although the propositions listed below are tentative hypotheses rather than scientific laws.

1 The more aware of their oppression in families and religion that women can become, the more able they will be to move toward their own freedom. Awareness of the facts of women's oppression is an essential first stage of women's empowerment.

2 Economic subordination must be neutralized for women to be empowered. One phase of women's efforts to increase their economic independence is to receive pay for the work that they do.

3 Women can advance their economic achievements in society by reducing their participation in domestic, unpaid work. Women cannot be all things to all people, and they cannot function effectively when they bear the burden of both family responsibilities and career goals.

4 When women educate themselves about women in other parts of the world, they gain a realistic perspective on their own lives. When they can go beyond the interpersonal stresses of their personal experiences to see the broader picture of subordination, they can be freer to pursue varied constructive achievements.

5 To the extent that women can feel unity with women in different cultural settings, they will be more open to receiving support and understanding from other women in their everyday lives. Increasing bonds between all women is a vital stage of women's empowerment.

6 Knowledge about worldwide trends in women's oppression increases the probability that informed women will not allow themselves to be defined by the same oppressive tendencies. Ignorance about women in the world at large guarantees that victimization. Patriarchies are not congenial to women, and only women can change the quality of women's lives. Men's vested interests in maintaining the status quo of patriarchal societies prevent them from seeing many of the problems that women experience, let alone working with women to accomplish real change on the behalf of women.

Chapter 9

Feminism and Value Choices

Feminism is an ideology or secular belief system that postulates that equality between the sexes is the only just and viable basis for effective social organization, productivity, and humanistic well-being (Bernard, 1981; Rowbotham, 1989). Feminism has inspired and undergirded a variety of social movements aimed at changing both people's behavior and their attitudes—especially their values (Carden, 1974; Smelser, 1986). From early declarations of the rights of women (Wollstonecraft, 1982) to contemporary feminist scholarship on the persistence of patriarchy, individual women and groups of women have tried to raise the consciousness of other women and of men to actively realize the ideal of freedom and equality for all (Ruth, 1980).

Feminists are realists as well as idealists. They frequently present their ideas and experiences in the context of male domination (Rowbotham, 1974), especially when repeated patterns in the subordination of women are increasingly documented throughout the world—findings that must be taken into consideration in any ideological formulation (Duchen, 1987; Evans, 1977; Kluckhohn & Strodtbeck, 1961). In fact, feminism is seen as one of the dynamic mechanisms of international social change (Chafetz & Dworkin, 1986; Firestone, 1971; Goode, 1963).

To the extent that ideals, ideas, and values modify social organization

(Cooley, 1962), feminism can be thought of as a powerful combination of assumptions and propositions (Beauvoir, 1974; Friedan, 1963, 1981). On a personal level, feminism can be a liberating experience for individual women (Mander & Rush, 1974), having the consequence of strengthening identities and participation in society as a whole (Diaz-Diocaretz & Zavala, 1985; Hall, 1990a).

Thus feminism can motivate women to orient their lives toward changing social structures (Gerth & Mills, 1946; Richardson & Taylor, 1983). By raising questions about religion and other established values (Daly, 1968, 1973; Hays, 1964; Plaskow, 1983), feminism also inspires scholarly research that describes and explains differences in women's and men's values (Andersen, 1988; Gilligan, 1982) and that extends understanding of human nature to include women's perspectives and experiences (Ruth, 1980). Feminism is a significant world view for women and for men. It draws attention to the fact that gender and patriarchy are established social institutions in almost all societies (Lengermann & Wallace, 1985).

To understand the impact of feminism on society, it is vital to highlight the ways in which patriarchy and beliefs in patriarchy have influenced people's construction of reality (Becker, 1950; Berger & Luckmann, 1966). At this basic level of defining reality, feminist perspectives are significant sources for the formulation of new paradigms that increase people's knowledge and understanding of human nature and human relations (Kuhn, 1970; Schaef, 1985).

Many of the issues that feminism explains or addresses through proposing solutions and directions for change are related to women's functions in society and in interpersonal relationships, including families (Chodorow, 1978, 1989; Coward, 1984; Greer, 1971; Mitchell, 1975; Richardson, 1988). Sometimes the suggested solutions are political and economic, as in socialism (Caute, 1967; Eisenstein, 1979), rather than responses to inner controls, which also have been defined as major barriers to women's freedom in contemporary society (Lengermann & Wallace, 1985).

Even with a variety of feminist ideologies from which to choose (Ruth, 1980), individual women may find it difficult to act from their own interests or embrace feminism as a cause (Mills, 1967). Women are much more heterogeneous in social situations than are men (Diaz-Diocaretz & Zavala, 1985), and it is crucial to discern the few vital, basic concerns that can both motivate and unite women (Rowbotham, 1989). Whether they are acted on in political terms or not, bonding and feelings of unity among women are sources of strength and support for women's empowerment.

LIFE HISTORIES

The following life histories illustrate how feminist ideology can empower individual women and lead toward women's collective empowerment. Whatever the education or social class of individual women may be, feminist ideology aims toward finding some shared basis of experience and concern among all women that can be a foundation for working toward the social good by bringing about more equal conditions for all.

Although the three examples given necessarily provide only a truncated view of each woman's understanding and application of feminism, the descriptions highlight similarities and contrasts in each woman's ability to act according to her own interests. Each woman experiences different consequences through actions based on feminism, just as each woman approaches life with a contrasting world view.

Nancy

Nancy is a Roman Catholic from a traditional, working-class, Irish-American family that does not question longstanding ways of doing things. As a youth, Nancy followed family traditions closely. With the full support of her family, she decided to pursue a teaching career, although she had some reservations about its appropriateness for her.

Nancy was introduced to feminism while she was in college. She took some women's studies courses and became involved in political activities of the women's caucus on campus. She began to see the world differently, and became seriously committed to the feminist view, applying feminist values and principles in her everyday life. However, to some extent, she was fearful of the consequences feminism might have for her future. She sensed that these new ideas would be unpopular with her family and even with her good friends. In spite of her apprehensions, Nancy proceeded to strengthen her interest in feminism. She increased her women's studies courses, as well as her participation in feminist political meetings.

As she had anticipated, Nancy had many conflicts with her parents. They eventually refused to pay for her education. Although Nancy was saddened by her parents' attitudes and actions, she did not stop incorporating feminist ideology and philosophy into her everyday life. She obtained work and student loans that enabled her to support herself and pay for her education.

Nancy had long been concerned about rape and other kinds of violence against women. After living with her new viewpoint, Nancy came to believe that crisis intervention work would make a more direct contribution to alleviating women's oppression than teaching. She changed her course of study to social work.

Nancy's new direction in her studies was satisfying to her, freeing her from the stress she had experienced about a career in teaching—which would have been a logical extension of her family's conservative values and her early upbringing, but about which she had strong reservations.

As Nancy learned more about international feminism, she came to realize the vast number and variety of ways in which women try to reduce unjust inequities between women and men. Feminism continues to have a significant impact on Nancy's life, through expanding her orientation to her own possibilities and her interaction with others. Feminist ideology has taken her out of the isolated, "obedient," accommodating posture her family trained her to have.

Violet

Violet is a 40-year-old black woman who is a physician in a suburban hospital. Until about a year ago, she had been so busy leading her professionally competitive work life that she had not paid attention to the ways in which she might have been treated differently by her colleagues because she is a woman.

It was not until she suffered from sexual harassment on the job that she began to look at her work situation more objectively, as well as her legal rights. She began to consider the feasibility of taking legal action against the proponent of her harassment.

After consulting a lawyer about these matters, Violet became aware that the harassment pattern of exploitation is experienced by many women in all ethnic groups and in all occupations. She became more alert to feminist articulations of women's rights and joined a nearby feminist political group that actively seeks legal reform in county and state governments. Although Violet did not have much knowledge about the existing laws against sexual harassment, she decided to work with her group to lobby for more effective legislation against this kind of objectification of women. She made a long-term commitment to accomplish this, and her dependability and sense of responsibility became an inspiration to all those who worked with her.

Violet's work situation changed for the better. The co-worker who had harassed her left the hospital and moved out of the area. However, because the man moved, it became more difficult for Violet to pursue her legal rights than it would have been if he had stayed in town.

Faced with a lack of reasonable legal recourse, Violet decided to move on with her life by working toward acquiring more knowledge about the problem of sexual harassment. She came to terms with the pain and humiliation of her own experience by trying to make changes that would help other women who go through this coercive infringement of their rights and humanity.

Grace

Grace is a 35-year-old white woman who is living on welfare. She has three children by different fathers and has never been married. For a time, she supplemented her restricted income with contributions from her current man friend, Jack, who paid for occasional room and board with which Grace provided him.

For many years, Grace did not have time to think about feminism or about educating herself about women's rights issues. She knew that her life was very difficult, but she did not particularly think of it as being influenced by social pressures.

Moreover, Grace was emotionally dependent on Jack. His attention relieved some of the stress she felt because of her weighty responsibilities as a parent with scarce means. Grace did not have much self-confidence, and she felt helpless about her current situation. She had never been able to hold down a job, and she had been disowned by her family.

When Grace did not do what Jack expected, he became violent. Grace put up with this "bad" side of Jack for some time, but eventually she became concerned that he would hurt her children.

Grace had nowhere to go to escape Jack's anger except to a city-run shelter for battered women. Although she did not make this move easily, she decided she had to protect herself and her family by going to the shelter.

While Grace was being cared for in the shelter, she learned a great deal from the other women living there. She began to see that her predicament was shared by many different women—including those with financial means—and she learned she had to empower herself in order to deal with her difficulties.

Grace did not become an ideologue because of her life-threatening experience and as a result of her gaining identification with other women. However, she became much more of a feminist than she had been before. Grace made enough progress in looking after her needs that she was able to find another place to live, as well as to hold down a part-time job. She continues to visit the women's shelter regularly to gain emotional support for her own and her family's needs, and to make a contribution to the welfare of other abused women.

ANALYSIS AND INTERPRETATION

Nancy, Violet, and Grace were able to make constructive, empowering changes in their lives through their openness to new ideas, especially those of feminism. They came to see that their own unique experiences were tied to other women's life situation concerns, and that changes are needed to improve the lives of all women, not just their own. Although Grace was the only one of these three women who was forced to make changes by a life-threatening situation, the circumstances Nancy and Violet experienced were sufficiently dramatic that they too were led to re-orient their lives and to address their own interests according to their newly cultivated feminist principles. Violet was able to add political activism to her already demanding professional life, and Nancy was able to move ahead with career plans based on her concern for equal rights for women.

Nancy had the courage to stand up to the immediacy of family pressures in order to take the direction in her life that she wanted most of all. Her parents' withdrawal of financial support was a major crisis for her, but she did not allow this event to paralyze her. She knew she had a meaningful purpose, and her own resourcefulness empowered her in the situation.

Nancy's feminism continues to be fairly intellectual, but this kind of interest works well for her. She feels that she is participating in a world revolution.

Violet's talents were directed toward feminist causes as a result of her professional humiliation. Because she had achieved so much in her professional career, she had mistakenly felt immune to the possibility of sexual harassment. Although she was aware that many women experience sexual harassment on the job, she thought that her status would insulate her from it.

Because Violet was an extremely talented and well-educated woman, it did not take her long to assess the social and political ramifications of sexual harassment. She plunged into organizational activities, lobbying for legislation to make the workplace safer for women. At the same time, faced with the realities of the legal system and her need to move on, she let go of her own harassment situation. Although this might not have been the most effective course of action for Violet to pursue in the long run, in terms of her sense of emotional fulfillment and personal dignity, it was the most common sense solution.

The violence in Grace's life prompted a kind of awakening or enlightenment for her. She had been unable to take steps to protect her own interest effectively until her physical safety—and the physical safety of her children—were threatened. Although Grace is not a very articulate woman, she had to express her pain to other women in order to gain control over her powerlessness. She received the support of other women and became a feminist because she wanted to return that help to others in need.

Nancy, Violet, and Grace were forced to make new kinds of value choices in their lives in order to get out of their own particular predicaments. Although everyone makes value choices continuously, their decisions—made in the spirit of feminism—were particularly significant for finding more security and meaning. Each of these women (especially Nancy and Grace) moved from being overly dependent on others to being more interested in making empowering changes in their lives and in the lives of others. They placed a stronger value on their own survival and well-being than they had been able to do earlier, and they looked for satisfactions that went beyond the shallowness of merely pleasing others.

CHOICES

Feminism directly and indirectly calls for political action on behalf of equality for women, and women must choose whether or not to answer this call. Some of the consequences of women's responses to feminism are suggested in the choices below.

1   When women choose to think of themselves as feminists, they see that women's collective welfare transcends one woman's individual need to be treated as equal.

2   Women's choices to act on behalf of women's interests give them new orientations. They see the world differently, and they interact with others in innovative ways.

3   When women deliberately choose to separate themselves from feminism, they unknowingly separate themselves from some of their own real interests. Although these women may choose not to express political ideology directly in their everyday behavior, their individual survival and well-being are ultimately connected to the lot of all women.

4   There are many kinds of feminism, and women may choose from among them. For example, women may choose to align themselves with artistic (rather than political) feminism. In fact, in some respects there are as many versions of feminism as there are women, but all forms of feminism ultimately lead toward the greater freedom of women and of men.

5   The more deliberately women choose feminism, the more directly feminism can influence their lives. However, a woman who chooses an antifeminist stand is still strongly influenced by feminism. Feminism is a reality that can be embraced or denied, but its existence persists.

6   Women who choose to participate in feminist activities find that they will be supported by other women. Mutual help is a significant aspect of women's empowerment.

GENERALIZATIONS

Acknowledging some of the patterns of feminism can enable individual women to decide more freely the extent to which they will choose to identify with the feminist movement. Although feminism claims to represent the interests of all women, many women—especially those in minority ethnic groups and lower social classes—do not experience feminism as a positive, supportive influence in their lives. Some of the generalizations that can be made about feminism as a worldwide political movement are noted here.

1   Although one of the explicit goals of feminism is to unite women and represent their collective interests, many women choose not to identify with this political movement. It is difficult for some women to see how their experiences can give them a meaningful orientation to specific objectives, such as reproductive rights.

2   Feminism in most countries has been led by middle-class, educated women. These mainstream women may appear to have very few values in common with lower-class women and women in minority ethnic groups. Weak organization in the women's movement stems largely from the lack of solidarity between the many heterogeneous groups of women that exist in any industrialized society. Women are much more heterogeneous than men; men tend to fall more easily into what is thought of as traditional social class distinctions.

3   Feminism is resisted by mainstream society, including women and men. This resistance does not negate or neutralize the influence of feminism, but it means that the expressed objectives of feminism will predictably be blocked by groups that have vested interests in maintaining the status quo.

4   Feminism has interpersonal and global implications and consequences. When equality is a central value of individual and social decisionmaking, waves of change emanate from small milieus to broader social structures. Women's empowerment through feminism has both intrapsychic and social consequences. Women's behavior changes at all levels of social organization due to the influence of feminist values.

5   Women may be more open to feminism at different stages of their lives. For example, as women grow older, they frequently become increasingly reflective, and they may find that they are able to review their life experiences in more meaningful ways through feminist interpretations. Thus, many women embrace different kinds of feminism at different times.

6   Feminism is a belief system that necessarily has the same kinds of limitations common to other belief systems. A true test for the viability of feminism is whether it serves as a meaningful guide and support for sufficient numbers of women in everyday circumstances. Facts show us that feminism is an increasingly effective philosophy for women; however, gaps exist between feminism as an ideal and its reality.

PROPOSITIONS

Women can understand the role feminism plays in social change more fully by delineating some of the correlations between feminist political ideology and women's collective action toward their equality. The propositions below suggest some of the ways in which feminism empowers women in both interpersonal and global settings.

1   To the extent that women are able to organize their efforts for equality through the ideology of feminism, they will be able to accomplish specific objectives such as legislative change. Because feminism is explicitly based on women's shared values, adherence to feminist ideology also increases the probability that women will agree on selected goals and means.

2   Feminism will increase its effectiveness by broadening its appeal expressly to include women from minority ethnic groups and lower social classes. This is difficult to accomplish because women's values differ, and women do not readily agree on the same long-term objectives for change.

3   The perspective of international feminism can increase women's inclinations to identify with each other. The broader the context of feminism, the larger will be the number of women that are represented by this ideology.

4   Feminism represents women's interests throughout their lives. When women see the relevance of thinking of themselves first and foremost as women when they conduct their daily business, the feminist belief system will serve as an increasingly dependable guide. Feminism is a world view that can be experienced and tested empirically by individual women. Only when feminism clearly enhances the quality of women's lives will it be deliberately embraced as an ideology or philosophy.

5 Feminism can be used as a mode of analysis for understanding behavior. Although this view of reality is limited, it can indicate the strength of the influence of gender in all social relations.

6 Women can be empowered with or without the conscious use of feminism. Feminism is an option that can benefit individual women and women as a group, but it is not a necessary or sufficient condition of women's empowerment. Feminism is a valuable support, which may or may not be used as a guide in decisionmaking and behavior.

Chapter 10

Empowerment

Women's empowerment includes both a personal strengthening and enhancement of life chances, and collective participation in efforts to achieve equality of opportunity and equity between different genders, ethnic groups, social classes, and age groups. It enhances human potential at individual and social levels of expressions. Empowerment is an essential starting point and a continuing process for realizing the ideals of human liberation and freedom for all.

Although a few people may still believe that conditions of equity will come into being through time, due to natural processes such as evolution (Alland, 1967), it is not readily apparent that justice can be achieved without a considerable degree of planned human cooperation. It appears necessary for women as the numerical majority of the population (Baxter & Lansing, 1983) to acknowledge and act on their potential strength by becoming a sufficient force to shape history (Beard, 1971).

When women see the world through perspectives that have different values, they construct new social realities (Berger & Luckmann, 1966). Feminism and research in women's studies provide women with innovative vantage points for conceptualizing and understanding reality. Women's realization that they have a direct impact on history, whether or not they participate directly in political activism, makes them more able to make a connection between their everyday experiences and broad trends. Biography and history are inextricably linked to each other, and women strengthen their individual and collective interests by acting fully in this knowledge (Berteaux, 1981; Mills, 1967).

Becoming increasingly aware of their own values can inhibit the automatic individual and social reaction women have to stereotype others, especially those they fear (Becker, 1950). However, when women become free of their conditioned attempts to blame or vilify others, they can find increased meaning in their everyday exchanges, as well as in their ideals and ideas (Blumer, 1969). Their very selves—their most intimate parts—are products of the values they cherish most and honor through their actions (Hall, 1990a).

When women choose positive values to characterize themselves (Luckmann, 1967), they neutralize the negative connotations others have bestowed on them (Hays, 1964). Women's minds and behavior may be oriented through the ideology of feminism (Mander & Rush, 1974; Mead, 1967; Weber, 1977). They can move forward to new levels of organization and being by recognizing their own potential as equals (Richardson & Taylor, 1983).

Women's empowerment frequently takes place at a personal level through their friendships with other women (Bell, 1981). Both extended family and community networks protect women (Bott, 1957), sometimes against violence and other life-threatening situations (Brownmiller, 1975). The strengthening of women's personal relationships also assists their growth and maturation (Cancian, 1987), making them more immune to their own debilitating and self-destructive patterns of behavior (Chernin, 1981). By deliberately counteracting social influences that condition them for dependent lives (Dowling, 1982), women can work effectively toward gaining access to power on domestic and international fronts (Epstein & Coser, 1981). Understanding the intricacies of personal relationships and everyday choices (Gerson, 1985; Glassner & Freedman, 1979; Hall, 1989, 1990b; Horner, 1972) is a vital starting point for forging roles of and avenues to power in the wider society (Lipmen-Blumen, 1984).

Women's gains in other countries serve as inspiration to national and local groups of women, even if the international achievements cannot be duplicated on home territory (Chafetz & Dworkin, 1986; Charlton et al., 1989; Evans, 1977; Flanz, 1983). Contrasting cultural values may make it difficult to understand women's status in different national settings (Kluckhohn & Strodtbeck, 1961), but increasing women's abilities to discern or to learn about particular patterns, such as discrimination, in other countries makes a needed contribution to their understanding of discrimination in general (Garcia de Leon, 1990).

Empowerment of ethnic groups in the United States (Staples, 1973) also can be expedited by seeing links between conditions in the United States and experiences in other countries, perhaps especially in other industrialized nations

(Charlton et al., 1989). Women's rights and human rights have consistent and persistent dimensions of reality, whatever the national context (Stetson, 1987).

Perhaps one of the clearest indicators of women's empowerment is an increase in women's capacities and willingness to support other women and to work diligently toward strengthening women in their efforts to survive or to gain equality (Bernard, 1971). It is only through acknowledging women's and men's interdependency in constructive ways (Durkheim, 1966) that women can enter into more powerful exchanges with men in society at large (Blau, 1967). Women's collective action is necessary to deal effectively with such important issues as violence against women (Hindberg, 1988), and the persistence of patriarchy in welfare states (Holter, 1984).

The probability of realizing women's freedom is increased through their awareness of the plight and possibilities they share with other women (Shibutani, 1955; Randour, 1987). When women are able to organize their efforts around crucial goals, such as changing particular values (e.g., prejudice against nontraditional feminine values) or specific behavior (e.g., discriminatory practices against women) in wider society (Smelser, 1962), women's empowerment will be realized more effectively.

LIFE HISTORIES

The biographical sketches of Sophie, Louise, and Jane given below illustrate different kinds of empowerment and the effects of these forms of empowerment on other people. Although empowerment is not synonymous with social class mobility, betterment of economic positions leads to greater empowerment. Increased economic independence and increased social contacts lead to being stronger and to having a stronger influence on others.

Sophie

Sophie is a white, middle-class, French woman who travels periodically to the United States. She is a journalist who aspires to work overseas for a major French newspaper. Although she was born and raised in a large family in a small town in France, she has learned much about women's rights through her university education and through living as a professional in Paris.

Sophie's visits to the United States have helped her gain perspective on her own life in France. She has become more aware of her professional opportunities by comparing her own experiences with those of women journalists in the United States. Although Sophie could not replicate or even approximate work conditions in her own office in Paris that are similar to conditions in the United States, she has become more objective about her rights and responsibilities by making comparisons between conditions in the two countries. Sophie's visits also have enabled her to see more clearly how her personal life supports or inhibits her professional accomplishments. Through deepening her understanding of how U.S. women conduct their personal lives, she has become more decisive about the range of options available to her.

Sophie's broadened perspective has enriched her life. She has a deeper affinity for other women and is less competitive with them on the job. She saves her energies for making constructive contributions toward improving women's working and living conditions. Her extensions of the boundaries of her personal and professional interests contribute toward the collective empowerment of women in France and in the United States.

Louise

Louise is a black, lower-class woman. She lives with her husband and two teenage daughters in the suburbs of a major city, and she attends a local Protestant church regularly.

For many years, Louise worked hard running her own small business, a flower shop. When she was 45 years old, she decided to go to college to earn a degree in business. Although she had gained a great deal of practical experience running her flower shop, she felt inadequate in specific office management skills. Also, Louise thought that having a business degree would open up more opportunities for growth than she would gain by continuing to run her flower shop.

Louise performed exceptionally well in her college studies, which was recognized by her professors, and her achievements came to the attention of her dean. Upon graduation, she was offered a responsible management position in the university admissions office. She decided to accept the position rather than continue to run her own business.

Louise's new work put her in touch with students, faculty, alumni, and students' families. She thrived on the extra social contacts and enjoyed campus life. In addition, she attended seminars on campus. After 6 months, she decided to study a master's degree in counseling. This credential would allow her to pursue her interest in communicating with people in professional ways.

Louise completed her counseling degree successfully, and she was recommended by her church for a position as a group leader of evening support programs held close to her home. Her example of strength gave much hope to others, and she inspired her clients, as well as her daughters, to make the most of their interest and skills. Louise's personal empowerment made her professional expertise more effective, and these accomplishments served others' needs as well as her own.

Jane

Jane is a white, lower-class woman who has lived most of her life in a small rural town. Her family has resided in this same town for many generations.

Upon graduating from high school, Jane was expected to go to work in one of the town's restaurants, as her mother and aunts had done before her.

Jane decided that the only way in which she could discover what life had to offer her was to leave her family. She moved out of the state, several hundred miles away, into the center of a major city.

Jane took an entry-level job in a bank in the city and worked hard for a promotion that would give her more permanent security. She became aware of women's issues through her observations on the job. She joined a local political group that supports the rights of women and gives her personal support. Jane became increasingly active in this group in her spare time, and she started to protect her position at the bank more carefully than she had done before.

Jane's life-style was now so different from that of her parents and family that when she visited their home she felt restricted and uncomfortable. However, in many respects, Jane's empowerment helped her younger sisters. They saw what she had accomplished professionally, and through her independence from the family.

Jane always returns to the city after her visits home with a deepened awareness of what it means to be her own self. She is more effective in accomplishing her goals than women who were raised not only in her home town, but also those raised in the city. Jane knows that she can measure the beginning of her empowerment from the time before she left her family. Although she has not been promoted through many levels at the bank, she is more than holding her own, and she has not been discriminated against overtly. Jane is confident that she can accomplish something with her life and can be recognized by others.

ANALYSIS AND INTERPRETATION

Sophie, Louise, and Jane are reflective women who can imagine themselves in positions of influence. They are objective about their situations, and they are able to take specific measures to free themselves from the restrictions and limitations inherent in their circumstances.

Sophie, Louise, and Jane are also decisive about their lives. They take risks and are able to leave familiar relationships and situations (either geographic or emotional) when appropriate. They extend their horizons and increase their contacts with others at the same time.

Sophie's geographic travels were more dramatic than those of either Louise or Jane. Travel permitted her to draw contrasts and make comparisons between conditions in France and the United States. Sophie incorporated some of the different cultural values of women from both countries into her own life. Sophie's experience of university education and living in Paris expanded her view of herself and her possibilities. Her increased cosmopolitanism helped her career in journalism. Because she no longer had a provincial attitude, her influence was felt and appreciated by increasing numbers of people.

Although Louise never experienced the drama of international travel, her adventurous undertaking to change her life brought about a marked shift in her social class position. She became a professional woman within a period of a few years, and this allowed her to give up the grueling responsibility of keeping her small, marginally profitable flower business alive.

Louise developed her innate interest in people during her undergraduate and graduate education. She chose a career in counseling, which provided her with opportunities to continue her many contacts with people. Louise's hard-won personal skills have translated effectively into professional techniques and accomplishments. She has not only become a counselor; she has become a constructively active participant in strengthening her own community.

Jane's most dramatic change was leaving her family and the small, rural town of her childhood. She performs impressively well in her city job at the bank, and she is able to empower herself more through her participation in the political women's group in her neighborhood.

Because she was sufficiently mature, Jane has maintained contact with her family throughout these changes. She finds that her trips home enable her to assess her life more effectively than if she stayed in the city continuously. Jane consistently returns to the city as a stronger person. She knows that she has changed a great deal since coming to the city, and she is willing and able to inspire other women in her family to make similar changes in their lives.

Jane's vigilance on the job prevents others from exploiting her as they could if she did not know her rights and responsibilities. Jane's co-workers depend on her a great deal, and she is considered to be one of the most promising young people working at the bank. These attitudes give Jane much confidence, and she feels certain that she can continue to empower herself in her working and living situations, and that she will do well in the future.

CHOICES

The first stage of women's empowerment at individual or social levels involves the process of reaching the decision to be empowered. Making this initial choice is a vital condition to all further action to be taken. Being open to the possibility of change is a necessary prerequisite for this basic change to become possible.

Some of the choices that women have to make to be empowered are listed below. Although many of these choices build on each other during the empowerment process, each choice has a degree of autonomy. Unless women reflect on these options seriously, it will be difficult for them to find meaning in their lives and to be fulfilled.

1 To become empowered, women must know what empowerment is and

believe that it is possible. The choice to see empowerment as an advantageous process precedes all other action to accomplish empowerment.

2 Women must choose to be responsible for their own thoughts, feelings, and behavior to become effectively empowered. Regardless of the support she may receive from others, it is not possible for anyone but a woman to empower herself. The assumption of this responsibility by each woman is a level of empowerment that is necessarily at the heart of all effective grassroots political activism.

3 Empowerment calls forth the choice for women to be connected to or optimally united with other women. Women's mutual support is a necessary condition of women's empowerment at individual and social levels.

4 Women must choose to identify with the experiences of women throughout the world. When women acknowledge that their own survival and fulfillment are dependent on the existing conditions for all other women, they will be freer and less subordinated by men.

5 Each woman must choose to see the broader picture of her life in order to be fully empowered. Women make wiser interpersonal and social decisions when they deliberately put their lives in as broad a context as possible.

6 Women's empowerment is based on each woman's choice to be aware of the facts in her life. When women see the reality of where they are and who other people think they are, they will be increasingly motivated to acknowledge who they are and become who they want to be.

GENERALIZATIONS

Women's empowerment tends to follow certain sequences and stages. When women are aware of these patterns in their own behavior and in their exchanges with others, they will be more able to become empowered on a long term basis. Empowerment inevitably meets with resistance. However, when women are prepared to see, handle, and understand this resistance, other people's resistance is more likely to be neutralized.

Some of the trends in women's individual and collective empowerment are listed below. Although different historical periods and contrasting cultural settings reveal vast differences in the lives of women, there are common denominators in their empowerment.

1 Women's empowerment is least developed in the most traditional patriarchal societies. Both interpersonal and collective levels of women's empowerment are inhibited by institutional hierarchical authority structures in traditional patriarchal societies.

2 Women's empowerment is a political process that must necessarily include individual decisionmaking. Women's collective empowerment cannot be achieved unless individual women make empowering decisions in their everyday interaction with others.

3 Women's empowerment is strongly influenced by class and ethnic group membership, but essentially these categories of stratification are functions of male hierarchical orders. They are not intrinsic to women's organizations. To the extent that women can truly act on the basis of their unity with all women, class and ethnic group memberships will lose some of their determining influences on women's lives.

4 Women's empowerment inevitably threatens the status quo in patriarchal societies. Resistance to women's empowerment is predictable, and the more prepared for resistance individual women can be, the more able to retain their empowerment they will be.

5 When women support each other in achieving independence and increasing options, their mutuality is empowering. Women achieve more when they can count on each other than when they act in isolation.

6 The development of creative strategies for women's empowerment— through discussion and collective problem-solving—is a short cut to empowerment that strengthens women's resources and effectiveness. Women's use of techniques of empowerment make it possible for them to organize themselves to act in their own interests.

PROPOSITIONS

Propositions highlight relationships between influences with which women have to deal to achieve empowerment. When women know the degree of their oppression in families, religion, work, and the world, they will become freer to formulate their goals for truly satisfying lives.

Propositions that describe and explain some aspects of women's empowerment are listed below. Although there are many complex phases and aspects of women's empowerment, these selected views represent a few of the most vital prerequisites for women's achievement of individual and collective empowerment.

1 To the extent that women can become independent in their families, they will be empowered in diverse social settings. Family pressures toward women's subordination are difficult to counteract, but when women can do so they will be able to maintain correspondingly more control of their behavior in nonfamilial settings.

2 To the extent that women can develop their own religious beliefs and practices within established denominational and sectarian orders, they will be motivated to work toward their equality and the well-being of all. Beliefs in a supreme being can empower women in the search for survival and fulfillment.

3 Women who increase their control over their work at home and outside the home are in advantageous positions for achieving equality and empowerment. Mutual support in work settings in and outside the home is vital to women's empowerment through work.

4 Increased knowledge about women's conditions throughout the world increases women's objectivity about their own conditions, and deepens their understanding of women's subordination. Having knowledge of this broader

world context of women's lives empowers women, in that they become more able to see their own historical and cultural circumstances.

5 To the extent that individual women connect their biographies with history, seeing the influence of broad social structures on their lives, they will be empowered. Social issues impinge on the quality of women's lives in their domestic milieus, and much of the distress that is thought of as interpersonal problems is the result of patriarchal social structures and institutions.

6 Women's mutual support is a necessary, but not a sufficient, condition of their empowerment. Alone, individual women cannot develop their potential or make their fullest possible contributions to society.

Chapter 11

Answers

Before drawing conclusions from this examination of the most significant aspects of women's empowerment and empowerment processes, some answers to the questions asked at the outset of this study can be suggested. Although all life history research is necessarily inconclusive, some tentative solutions to women's subordination appear feasible through more fully understanding the influences of self, gender, family, religion, work, world, and feminism in women's empowerment.

In many respects, the findings here are discouraging. The traditional objectification of women persists at all levels of social organization (Cohn, 1989; Della Fave, 1980; Sanday, 1981). In spite of overwhelming evidence substantiating the facts of women's subordination, the social sciences are slow to incorporate gender concerns into the mainstream of their disciplines (Gordon, 1988; Kandal, 1988; Rosenberg & Turner, 1981). As a consequence of what is essentially a trivialization of the influence of gender throughout society, gender is understood to be merely one of many undifferentiated influences in social change (Mannheim, 1936; Tiryakian, 1981; Wallace, 1989).

However, to the extent that new emphasis is given to delineating the influence of gender at all levels of social organization, it will be possible to produce more adequate sociological theories (Chafetz, 1990; Coleman, 1988; Curtis & MacCorquodale, 1990). Feminist theory and substantive findings will feed into qualitatively new conceptualizations and paradigms in the social sciences (Malson et al., 1989; Sydie, 1987).

In order to understand fully the impact of gender in personal and public lives, life history data must be taken more seriously in scientific endeavors (Berger, 1990). Women's worlds need to be incorporated into a collective understanding of human nature (Kandal, 1988), and gender relations research will have to be synthesized to represent the interplay between both microsociological and macrosociological concerns (Rosenberg & Turner, 1981; Sieber, 1974; Tiryakian, 1981).

Perhaps the most consistent finding in this study is that, in spite of changes in attitudes, there are many persistent themes in contemporary gender relations. When attention is given to gender variables, more is learned about stability and enduring institutionalization than change (Chafetz, 1990; Curtis, 1986). In addition to these clear continuities (Kandal, 1988), the variations that have been documented in attitudes, behaviors, and social structures will have to be accounted for in the development of new theoretical paradigms needed to describe and explain human nature (Rosenberg & Turner, 1981; Tiryakian, 1981).

DO WOMEN AND MEN EXPERIENCE SELF DIFFERENTLY?

The worlds of women and men have historically been different, and they continue to be different. When women examine their real selves, they find a gap between their own experiences and the institutionalized expectations of men (Turner, 1976). To the extent that women can bridge this gap by acting with a reliable knowledge of the social structures in which they find themselves and, at the same time, act in accordance with their own integrity, they will be empowered. A synthesis of the microsociological and macrosociological aspects of women's lives, through their own life history circumstances (Berger, 1990), will enable women to neutralize their programming and become more autonomous (Franks & McCarthy, 1989; Hewitt, 1990).

Although the selves of both women and men are affected directly by the economy (Zaretsky, 1976), women's and men's values also allow economic influences to have a major impact on the quality of their lives. However, when women value their economic resources and assets more, they will be more able to empower themselves by acting from a position of equality.

TO WHAT EXTENT DOES GENDER INFLUENCE BEHAVIOR?

It appears that gender socialization permeates all levels of social exchanges (Dinnerstein, 1976). Learned gender behavior is a powerful determinant of unequal relations between the sexes (Estep, 1977; McCall & Simmons, 1978). Broad social structures and institutions magnify these imbalances in interpersonal behavior (Cohn, 1989; Gutek, 1985; Kanter, 1977).

One implication of the persistence of learned gender differences is that if socialization processes can be changed in critical ways, adaptation that involves shifts in macro structures at later stages may occur (Mason et al., 1976; Millett, 1970; Sanday, 1981). However, it is disheartening to note that resistance to women's changes is ever-present. In light of attempted changes, the experience of many societies has been to overwhelmingly maintain existing patterns of the traditional subordination of women (Pescatello, 1973).

One avenue of possible significant change, given the pervasiveness of gender influences, is the workplace outside the home. To the extent that equality can be effectively legislated in the workplace, there may be shifts in attitudes and behavior in other spheres of social life (Hewitt, 1990; Matthaei, 1982; Rosen, 1989). When greater equality is actually accomplished, androgynous models of human nature can substitute for some of the traditional expectations for women and men (Coleman, 1988), giving rise to new modes of stability (Curtis & MacCorquodale, 1990).

IS THE FAMILY THE PRIMARY SITE OF WOMEN'S OPPRESSION?

For most women in most of the world, it appears that the family remains the most significant site, and even source, of oppression. In spite of the occurrence of any changes in society at large, household tasks and parenting continue to assume a traditional cast in the gender division of labor (Curtis, 1986). Because most of women's emotions are invested in their programming to be the primary caretakers for the family (Estep, Burt, & Milligan, 1977; Franks & McCarthy, 1989), it is very difficult to accomplish changes in these patterns of attitudes and behavior in the domestic sphere (Coleman, 1988).

In societies and circumstances where the most shifts have occurred that free women from being overburdened by their domestic responsibilities, women's work outside the home may become a liberating factor for women by providing them with independent economic means (Rosen, 1989). All too often, however, women continue to be burdened by their work both in and outside the home, and the family remains a primary site of women's oppression (Bradley, 1989; Sieber, 1974).

CAN WOMEN BE EMPOWERED THROUGH RELIGION?

As long as life history data support the hypothesis that religion empowers many women, there is a possibility that broad changes will make women less oppressed by institutionalized religion and by their formal roles in denominational and sectarian religions. However, religion is an emotionally charged arena of behavior, and broad changes will necessarily be slow to occur (Franks & McCarthy, 1989).

International data suggest that religion remains an oppressive force for women in the world at large (Lindsay, 1980). Because there have been and are so few women leaders to instigate change on national and international levels, the persistence of these patterns appears to be likely. However, to the extent that grassroots activism is based on the individual decisionmaking of individual women, empowerment can occur at individual and collective levels.

CAN WOMEN BE FULFILLED THROUGH THEIR WORK?

Only when women are not overburdened by their work can they be fulfilled through their work. As economic realities make work outside the home a necessity for contemporary women in the United States and other highly industrialized countries (Peterson, 1989), a shared, increased valuing of women's work is imperative (Reskin, 1988). The hidden aspects of women's work must be acknowledged and rewarded (Bose, Feldbera, & Sokoloff, 1987; Kessler-Harris, 1981), and equal access to positions of power will have to be forged and reforged (Kanter, 1977).

When women gain social recognition and their own senses of achievement in community settings, they will be more motivated to accomplish structural changes for other women (Rosen, 1989). The current burdensome aspects of women's working outside the home slows this effort (Levy, 1989; Sieber, 1974), and resistance to women's advancement persists (Gutek, 1985).

ARE WOMEN IN OTHER COUNTRIES DIFFERENT FROM WOMEN IN THE UNITED STATES?

In spite of marked contrasts in cultural values and levels of economic development, women's experiences have basic similarities throughout the world. Caste-like characteristics exist in some societies (Lindsay, 1980), and some gender equality has been achieved in other societies (Spiro, 1979). Traditional expectations about women and families remain, however, and these may or may not be overcome by individual women, by different social classes and ethnic groups of women, and by women in general (Levy, 1989; Pescatello, 1973).

Perhaps one advantage of the omnipresent subordination of women throughout the world is that it can become the basis of a new kind of international feminism. However, it is very difficult for women to feel a kinship with those women who are either less or more fortunate than themselves. A groundswell of support for international feminism is not likely to occur, given current levels of communication and education (Malson, O'Barr, Wihl, & Wyer, 1989). Perhaps acknowledging women's differences—and, as already stated, women are a much more heterogeneous group than men—will be one way to at least address the issue of where to draw the line between shared experiences and social and economic contrasts (McKinney & Sprecher, 1989).

DOES FEMINISM INCREASE OR DECREASE WOMEN'S EMPOWERMENT?

To the extent that feminism heightens women's awareness and increases the bonding between women, feminism increases women's empowerment. However, when feminism distorts facts and intensifies militancy, it can disorient women and lead to diverse kinds of resistance (Levy, 1989).

Feminism can be a useful vehicle for women to expedite their examination of their identities and interactions (McCall & Simmons, 1978). Analyses of values can show how sexual relations and gender relations can be viewed as issues of power (Millett, 1970; Sydie, 1987; Wallace, 1989). The new visions of society generated by feminism can be significant for social change (Mannheim, 1936), as long as these views are in touch with reality (Fitzpatrick, 1990).

On an individual level, feminism can be a support for women who are trying to make changes in their personal lives (Oliker, 1989). Although most of the problems that women face are structural (Della Fave, 1980) and, therefore, difficult for individual women to overcome, women's examinations of the role of gender in their own socialization can have some important individual and social liberating effects (Estep, Burt, & Milligan, 1977; Hewitt, 1990).

WHAT DOES WOMEN'S EMPOWERMENT ACHIEVE?

Women's empowerment helps women to make necessary transitions over their life courses (Foner & Kertzer, 1978; Marks, 1977). As the patterns of women's interactions have an impact on broader social structures, to the extent that they make changes in these exchanges, they will be in more advantageous positions to make changes at broader levels of social organization (Sanday, 1981).

When women find their real selves, they will be more able to recognize that many of the institutional demands on them are alien to their true interests (Turner, 1976). Empowering changes in women's attitudes result in new values that motivate them to participate more actively in broader social contexts (Mason, Czajka, & Arber, 1976; Roper & Labeff, 1977).

Women's empowerment allows women to be appreciated and acknowledged for who they are and what they do (Kessler-Harris, 1981; Levy, 1989). Women's support of other women (Oliker, 1989) heralds a new stage of women's development, where women can unite and act collectively to reduce and remove oppressive social structures (Fitzpatrick, 1990).

On both individual and social levels, women's empowerment neutralizes and sometimes negates their pervasive devaluation (Reskin, 1988). Women's empowerment also modifies women's existing sexual ideologies (Mason & Bumpass, 1975) by introducing women's own goals and values into their decisionmaking. Women become more autonomous through their empowerment and, consequently, institutionalized patterns of gender arrangement will continue to be scrutinized and questioned.

Chapter 12

Conclusion

Women are empowered when they are in touch with their own traditions, shared achievements, and real interests (Schaef, 1985). Women's expansion of power depends on their abilities to stay centered in their own uniqueness, as well as to be open simultaneously to the range of action possibilities demonstrated through other women's lives (Gerson, 1985).

Women's personal exchanges with other people are unavoidably influenced by their historical circumstances. Women act most effectively when they can recognize the inevitability of this interdependence of influences and can formulate their goals on the basis of this interdependence (Hall, 1990a).

It is not particularly the ideology of feminism that empowers women, but rather their capacities to face bravely the individual and social facts of their actual situations (Lengermann & Wallace, 1985). Through examining the facts of their lives, women understand themselves and their circumstances more fully and become freer of the external and internal controls that would otherwise define their lives for them. This process of empowerment also may be thought of as the way in which women observe, interpret, and assess their realities as objectively as possible (Andersen, 1988).

Empowerment allows women to move beyond others' conventional gender stereotypes and rigid gender role definitions (Scott, 1982). When women deliberately turn toward the most significant sites of their oppression—families, religion, and work—they begin to see the complexities and nuances of their own exploitation (Mills, 1967). Women must know themselves sufficiently to become freer, and this occurs only when they understand how much society controls them and perpetuates their subordination (Randour, 1987).

Feminist ideology can increase women's identification with each other (Richardson & Taylor, 1983). A primary goal of feminism is to promote women's organization for collective action worldwide. This social movement of feminism ostensibly gives meaning and direction to women's efforts to rectify the many different kinds of social injustices against women (Chafetz & Dworkin, 1986).

However, there is a possible danger in women's immersion in the ideology of feminism: individual women may lose their vital uniqueness within the intensity of the solidarity of women's political movements (Rosenberg, 1979). Feminism is essentially a means to achieve a particular kind of social organization, rather than a mode of personal expression. Whereas collective action is generally more effective if it has an ideological component, and most viable social movements have ideological underpinnings, individual behavior can be misdirected or distorted through an excessive ideological orientation and motivation (Schur, 1984).

Regardless of whether feminism exerts a strong influence on women's lives, belief systems in general frequently define the behavior of individual women and women as a group (Berger & Luckmann, 1966; Weber, 1977). Although every human being is usually much more than she or he believes (Cooley, 1964), people are strongly motivated to act through the beliefs and values they hold about themselves, others, and the world, however inaccurate those beliefs may be (Kluckhohn & Strodtbeck, 1961). People tend to do what they believe they can do, although they may be capable of more than they believe they are (Hall, 1990a).

When women make their own empowerment into a goal close to their hearts—a primary task of each day—they will inevitably become an integral part of grassroots activism (Diaz-Diocaretz & Zavala, 1985; Iglitzin & Ross, 1986). However, when women choose to ignore or deny their need to be empowered, they become pawns of the social mechanisms that perpetuate their subordination (Durkheim, 1984).

The first stage of women's empowerment is women's awakening to the facts of their existence—throughout the United States, in different ethnic groups, in different social classes, and in the world around them (Charlton, Everett, & Staudt, 1989). Empowerment is the initial phase of women's liberation, freedom, and equity, as well as a long-range goal of women's political participation. It is the first step in a long journey toward the formulation and realization of human rights and responsibilities that transcend gender role ste-reotypes and the objectification of women and of men.

As we have not yet arrived at a constructively balanced reciprocity between women and men (Blau, 1967; Pleck, 1985), women have much to learn from other minority groups' experiences in trying to achieve equal rights (Davis, 1983; Wilson, 1980). Also, when women understand their past and present roles in history more fully (Beard, 1971), they will recognize society's resis-tance to assimilating women's values into established knowledge (Kuhn, 1970) and see the critical roles women play in the dialectic of evolution (Alland, 1967).

CREATING NEW KNOWLEDGE

Facts of the individual life histories described in this book reflect the experi-ences of all women. Personal exchanges in women's lives are inextricably re-lated to their interaction on the job and to the development—or lack of development—of their careers. Furthermore, women's views of themselves are frequently and unwittingly influenced strongly by how others see them.

Given the social interdependence of women's and men's behavior, it is necessary to understand women more fully to really understand men and to deepen the understanding of human nature in general. Most current knowledge is based on the experience of men rather than women (e.g., there are more male researchers and more male subjects of research), so what knowledge is achieved is inevitably distorted unless it deliberately incorporates women's ex-periences and research into conceptualizations and explanations of reality. Women's reports of their life histories show that the social structures and oppor-tunities that define women's lives are qualitatively different from those that define the lives of men.

In accumulating data to generate new knowledge about women, it is impor-tant to be familiar with both subjective and objective dimensions of women's realities. Life history data are particularly useful in this respect. They provide impressionistic facets of women's experiences, as well as the bare facts of their existence. The profiled abstracts of information about what happens over long periods of time give longitudinal data, rather than a truncated cross-section of information, which would be characteristic of more conventional survey re-search.

One finding from the accumulation of new information about women's lives is that these lives show differences from the lives of men that make resulting knowledge suspect to male-dominated established interests. As women and men generally live in separate empirical worlds, it is difficult to have this new knowledge about women accepted and treated as seriously as knowledge about men.

APPLICATIONS

One way to prove the usefulness of new knowledge about women is to apply the essence of these findings to the lives of women who want to make changes in their lives. Identity empowerment theory, a clinical sociological theory, is an example of how a series of concepts can be derived largely from women's experiences and then applied to the lives of both women and men (see Appendix I for a more detailed description of identity empowerment theory).

Women who experience crises in their personal lives can be helped constructively by being encouraged to see the broader picture of their lives. All too often, women's interpersonal struggles—with other women and men—are not fueled by conflict from within relationships, but rather by the impact of the values and social controls of basic social institutions. In this study of women's empowerment, family, religion, and work were examined more closely than other factors, because pressures from these three social institutions historically have trapped women in segregated and subordinate roles more profoundly than other social structures.

Although women define themselves through their work to as great a degree as men do, one significant means through which women are filtered into the workplace is through their family conditioning. An examination of family pressures and expectations reveals how much pressure is placed on women to stay in a division of labor that gives women total responsibility for the day-to-day management of the family. Not only are women held responsible for child care, but also for the care of the elderly. Furthermore, regardless of women's work responsibilities outside the home and the income that their work generates, they are still expected to accept demanding in-home duties.

Another powerful source of women's conditioning for subordinate lives is religion. Although women may be motivated to pursue particular work as a vocation through their religion, as men are, women's roles in most religious settings are to obey and be devoted to the traditions of the religion and the family. Religion endorses family expectations, because religion needs to recruit its new members through the families who participate in their congregations.

When women can look objectively at the strengths and weaknesses of their conditioning by families and religion, they are in stronger positions to be independent. When they realize how some women have opened up their lives—as shown in the examples of empowerment in the life history data given in this volume—they, too, can follow suit, taking the risks necessary for their own empowerment.

FUTURE PATTERNS

It is almost impossible to predict specific trends in the U.S. population and much less possible to predict international trends. But it is to be hoped that society will experience and allow for more equality and equity between women and men in the future than it does at present. Valuable human resources are wasted whenever there is oppression and exploitation. Each woman's life is the heart of a grassroots activism that is necessary for the individual and collective empowerment of all women.

Because women's values are heterogeneous—differing widely across social classes and ethnic groups—it is predictable that men will resist the addition of those values to their own established system of more homogeneous values. Although overt conflict between women and men is not inevitable, on either the personal or public levels of society, it is likely that some of the value differences will be expressed as pressures, controls, and disagreement, as well as violence.

A precondition of women's empowerment is that increasing numbers of women must be prepared to help and support other women. It is not sufficient that men "allow" or legislate women's equality. Women need to be able to count on women in all circumstances. Only when this willingness to be there for other women is achieved will women's empowerment have a sufficient impact on society to improve the quality of life for all.

CHOICES

Women must make several choices in order to assess the usefulness and meaningfulness of empowerment. Also, women must make choices that are predictably effective in order to maintain their empowerment. Some of the choices women must consider are listed below.

1 In order to be empowered, women must want to be empowered. Although it may be comfortable to live dependently for a short time, sooner or later women must address the issue of becoming independent and make deliberate choices in one direction or another.

2 Choosing to be one's real self and choosing to develop one's potential are synonymous with the choice to be empowered. Empowerment has many phases, and choosing actions that constructively build one's resources is one aspect of an overall empowerment that must be continuous in order to be effective.

3 Choosing to lead a meaningful life will eventually lead to empowerment. Women must be sufficiently courageous to ask basic questions about the quality of their lives in order to live fully and productively.

4 The choice to be empowered needs to be renewed continuously. Empowerment is a process that has to be forged at all stages of the lifecycle.

5 The accomplishment of women's empowerment does not mean that others will necessarily be oppressed. When women choose their own empowerment, they are in stronger positions to support others and to make more solid contributions to society.

6 Empowerment requires women to face the facts of their lives at all levels of social organization. Choosing to be realistic in interpersonal and community matters is essentially the choice to be empowered.

GENERALIZATIONS

In order to stay empowered, women will have to be familiar with at least some of the institutional trends that had previously restricted them. Knowing what to expect from others in the course of their empowerment will enable women to maintain stronger functioning positions.

Some of the generalizations that can be made about women's empowerment as a social change process are listed below. The welfare of one woman remains inextricably tied to the welfare of all women.

1   Women's empowerment is a social process that neutralizes women's oppression. If women do not take decisive action on their own behalf, their victimization will continue automatically through their traditional subordination.

2   Grassroots political activism growing from women's empowerment derives from women's decisions to be empowered. The actions that follow women's resolves for empowerment create new patterns of interdependency that allow women to develop their potential and to take broader roles in community and societal activities.

3   Women's empowerment is synonymous with the achievement of equity and equal mindedness in society. These are not accomplished at the expense of others, but in a mutually cooperative spirit wherever possible.

4   Women's empowerment will result in traditional female values being more respected in society at large. It is not women's purpose to take power from men; rather, the goal of women is to develop their own power while respecting men for who they are.

5   Women's empowerment is a base for human liberation and empowerment for all. Although initially women will neutralize patriarchal structures in order to ground their own rights in social realities, women cannot be empowered effectively at the expense of others.

6   Women's empowerment will bring more balance to the male value hierarchies in current traditional and modern societies. Empowerment reestablishes cooperation as a viable social process and makes the development of all people more possible than is the case in fiercely competitive patriarchies.

PROPOSITIONS

Propositions relate directly, if hypothetically, to patterns of predictability in society. The propositions below suggest some strategies for women who want to empower themselves, as individuals or as a group.

1   The more empowered women become, the stronger the resistance this empowerment will initially produce. However, in the long run, women's empowerment will bring balance and not disruption to social relations.

2   Whether individual women or groups of women pursue their empowerment, social resistance is predictable. Empowerment will continue to be feasi-

ble only if women continue working in the direction of their own goals. If they capitulate, women will move back into their positions of subordination.

3 Women's empowerment moves women in the direction of living more fully. The more empowered women are, the more fully they live, and the more meaningful their lives become.

4 To the extent that women's empowerment increases in a particular social class or cultural setting, those women who are empowered will necessarily depend on other women for their well-being. Not until all women move out of their subordination will all women be truly empowered.

5 Women's work outside the home can be a primary avenue of their empowerment. When women have economic independence, they will be able to take firmer stands against their oppression in families.

6 If women can integrate their needs for empowerment with their religious beliefs, their motivations for empowerment will intensify. Women's collective mission includes expressing their real selves in order to neutralize existing restrictive patriarchal structures and to build a truly new world.

Identity Empowerment Theory

Identity empowerment theory is a recently developed clinical sociological theory that has been built on documented patterns and predictabilities in interpersonal, family, and group behavior (Hall, 1990b). It is used as an integrated frame of reference throughout *Women and Empowerment*, although this practice is not explicitly stated in all analyses, interpretations, generalizations, and propositions.

Identity empowerment theory describes and begins to explain critical clinical and social processes that increase the probabilities and possibilities of women's well-being and optimal functioning. The theory is grounded in the assumption that empowered women make meaningful commitments and undertake effective, goal-oriented activities that they choose for themselves.

METHODOLOGY

The 10 sociological concepts of identity empowerment theory derive from life history data that have been collected by the author in clinical and research settings over a 20-year period. Most of the interviews conducted lasted for 1 hour, and a question-and-answer format with one or two respondents was used. Although women of all ages, all social classes, and all ethnic groups were interviewed, the sample was not systematically representative of the U.S. population. Most of the respondents in both clinical and research interviews were white, middle-class women.

Approximately 500 detailed life histories—from the author's clinical practice and research in this 20-year period—were compiled and examined. Twenty-four life histories were selected from the total pool of life history data, expressly to illustrate the main themes of *Women and Empowerment*. In some cases, data were combined to create the profiles presented in *Women and Empowerment*.

Three quarters of the interviews conducted by the author took place in a clinical setting. The primary purpose of those interviews was to provide pertinent information for effective clinical interventions. One quarter of the interviews conducted by the author took place in a research setting. The primary purpose of those interviews was to collect data to describe and explain identity empowerment, particularly women's empowerment.

A wide range of open-ended questions was used in both the clinical and research settings, so that richly detailed information could be collected and examined closely. In the clinical interviews, follow-up probe questions about clients' personal beliefs and values, such as those related to religion, were used where clients were willing and interested in discussing these topics (Hall, 1991). Sometimes up to 40 hours of successive 1-hour interviews were held with clients. These meetings were scheduled at intervals that ranged from 2 weeks to 1 month.

In order to use life history data effectively in clinical practice, the most significant patterns of behavior in each person's life course were delineated from the accumulated information recorded. The basic methodology of asking questions and recording answers generated vast substantive sources, from which the concepts of identity empowerment theory were continuously reformulated and applied to describe and explain individual women's empowerment.

Twenty-five percent of the life history data collected for *Women and Empowerment* derives from research interviews. The question-and-answer format used in these research interviews does not vary significantly from the format of the clinical interviews. The most marked difference in the research interviews was their problem-free orientation. Present crisis was not necessarily a concern for the respondents in research interviews, and none of the research subjects was selected or initiated contact with the researcher for the purpose of solving particular interpersonal or family problems.

Research subjects were interviewed over the 20-year period on a volunteer basis, with subjects who had an interest in identity or identity empowerment. Most of the research interviews were conducted on a single occasion, although some follow-up interviews were held with the same subjects at different times during the 20-year period.

The questions used in the research interviews focused on the subjects' perceptions and participation in their families, religion, education, and work. Issues of personal transformation, commitments, and decisionmaking were addressed or explored in the research interviews. These issues frequently included topics such as how subjects' world views, values, and behavior had changed during a decade or throughout their lives.

Generally, research interviews were held with only one or two subjects at the same time and sometimes lasted less than a full hour. When respondents were particularly interested in questions about values and beliefs, probe questions were used to gather more detailed information, as in the clinical consultations.

In addition to formal data collection through clinical and research interviews, the author also participated in groups where women presented their life histories to other women. In addition to participating in these general mutual support women's groups, the author organized women's discussion groups with a specific women's empowerment theme over a 5-year period. The women's empowerment discussion meetings were held for 1.5 hours on a monthly basis, and the number of participants ranged from 5 to 15. Women of all ages, social classes, and ethnic groups participated in these discussions.

CONCEPTS

The 10 concepts of identity empowerment theory essentially become clinical tools or perspectives during crisis interventions. They are used to broaden the contexts through which women define themselves, their situations, and their life chances, thus linking the personal and public aspects of their lives.

These concepts can be thought of as ever-expanding views of self within society. In order to accomplish this broadened perspective, the scope of the concepts cuts across both personal milieus and the broader social structures and institutions of society.

Identity empowerment theory proposes that adult growth is an opening up of the perceived and behavioral worlds in which people live. Everyday social interaction is thought of as negotiations of values that emphasize the working notion that people are who they are and they do what they do due to the beliefs and values they cherish most (Berger & Luckmann, 1966; Blumer, 1969; Cooley, 1964; Goffman, 1973; Homans, 1961).

When individuals trade values with each other (Pruitt, 1981), negotiating strategies and resulting behavior depend on the significance or emotional importance the particular values have to each person involved in the negotiation (Strauss, 1978). Because differences in values are a common occurrence, many values may be compromised in negotiations with other people. However, if people take a stand based on their values, others are forced to adapt or leave those relationships. Heightened self-awareness, which implies a general consistency in value commitments, is the basis of a person's strongest negotiating position and most meaningful source of motivation.

Identity empowerment can be initiated in many different ways. Women heighten their awareness of how values and goals influence their lives at varied levels of experience and interaction. Identity empowerment enhances women's capacities to take value stands in their own interests in personal and public negotiations.

The 10 sociological concepts of identity empowerment theory bridge micro- and macrostructures, synthesizing subjective and objective dimensions of social reality. Each concept is a context or dimension of individual and social realities.

Women are able to scrutinize the impact of social structures and other social influences on their self-concepts and life experiences by deliberately focusing on each concept of identity empowerment theory. The structure of this frame of reference allows women to reflect on their lives more objectively than free-wheeling discussion allows, and the end-product—their identity empowerment—is a clarification and strengthening of their perceptions of themselves and society. Identity empowerment and women's mutual empowerment are essentially processes through which women consolidate their resources for everyday negotiations of values with others and increase the effectiveness of their collective action toward goals in their own interests.

Self

Self-awareness and self-knowledge are preconditions of identity empowerment and the initiation of new patterns of behavior. No significant change in behavior can occur without a thorough examination of habitual patterns of behavior, particularly those that include intimates and authority figures. This scrutiny uncovers people's deepest priorities and preferences.

Women's personal histories are outcomes of successful or failed expressions of integrity and compromises, as well as evidence of impasses and conflicts in their value negotiations. A focus on self enables women to decide which values they cherish most and which they want to claim as their own for future negotiations with others.

Although attitudes and behavior are directly related to micro- and macrostructures, few people have the requisite objectivity—or even the desire—to understand the strength and implications of this connection. However, women's discussions can shed light on these complexities, as well as further their understanding of their own situations.

Dyad

Dyads are two-person, intrinsically unstable relationships. A dyad is the basic unit of analysis in exchange theory (Blau, 1967).

Examinations of the variety of routinized dyads in which people participate are essential for delineating habitual behaviors at all levels of analysis and organization. Patterns of superordination, subordination, symbiosis, and less extreme dependencies need to be examined in order to determine which patterns are the most characteristic for certain individuals and groups and which carry the highest degree of emotional significance.

Triad

The most stable microstructure in which an individual participates is a triad (Caplow, 1968; Wolff, 1950). Participation in a triad is generally made up of patterns of dyadic closeness or conflict with a third-party outsider. The outsider position is preferred when the two other parties are in conflict rather than emotionally close to each other. In all cases, the outsider has the most autonomy and the strongest functioning position (Bowen, 1978; Kerr & Bowen, 1988).

Because a triad cannot easily sustain balance or equilibrium through the protracted equal participation of all its members, an outsider is less restricted than the dyadic participants. The members of dyads tend to interact in recurring dependent patterns of closeness or conflict—cycles that cannot be broken easily.

Dyadic interaction is intensified—positively or negatively—through the relative detachment of the third party. Autonomy from the emotional claims of members of dyads provides opportunities for third parties to empower self, through actions and commitments that express their preferred values in broader social contexts. Identity empowerment also enables people to stay in the strong outsider positions of their triads.

Family

Traditional family relationships, defined by kinship or contract, are meaningful emotional bonds for most people. However, alternative support groups may serve a similar emotional function to that provided by families, and long-standing friendships are sometimes absorbed into family emotional systems.

Families may be thought of as being relatively open or closed emotional systems, and membership may include relatives from several generations (Bowen, 1978; Kerr & Bowen, 1988). A family is the most intensely dependent lifetime group to which an individual belongs.

Religion

In identity empowerment theory, religion is defined broadly to include people's most fundamental beliefs and assumptions about the supernatural and reality, as well as conventional denominational or sectarian beliefs. Everyday beliefs and organized traditional religious beliefs are both frequently tied to institutional structures (Berger & Luckmann, 1966).

Traditional and modern religious beliefs, as well as secular beliefs, exert strong influences on clients' perceptions of themselves, others, society, and the universe.

Identity empowerment requires an examination of one's internalized religious beliefs. Women are encouraged to make more deliberate choices to accept or discard specific religious beliefs in the empowerment process. New beliefs about self and others, as well as new religious or value commitments, are formulated and embraced while doing this.

Definition of the Situation

Women's definitions of their own life situations provide a crucial subjective link between their self-understanding and their perceptions of society. Their subjective views of social realities result from their emotional adherence to particular values. Through a focus on the definition of the situation process, women can redefine problematic aspects of their living conditions as opportunities for change.

Redefining life situations is a value-laden activity for women. Optimally, women should select orienting values that expand their perceptions of their current situations, thereby facilitating constructive changes in these conditions. Beliefs about self and reality are influential motivating forces that have significant social consequences (Thomas, 1931). Therefore, identity empowerment necessarily includes clients' self-conscious and deliberate redefinitions of all aspects of the situations of their everyday lives.

Reference Group

Reference groups are desired status groups that may be achieved, such as professional associations, or ascribed status groups of sex or ethnicity. Women's behavior is influenced by the intensity of their sense of belonging to groups that have specific meaning for them. It matters little whether women actually belong to reference groups or merely aspire to group memberships.

Life history data over long time periods or during transitions in social mobility show changing sequences of subjective and objective affiliations with reference groups (Merton & Kitt, 1969). Identity empowerment results from women's increased awareness of the influence of their commitments to valued reference groups on their behavior.

Class

All micro- and macrosociological structures and processes are anchored in social classes. Social classes are socioeconomic strata or groups with the same vested interests (Dahrendorf, 1959). Classes also may be based on age, gender, race, and ethnicity (Hess, Markson, & Stein, 1988).

Classes are not formally organized and have many members who are unaware of their class affiliation or class designation by others. Whether or not women have previously considered what their class memberships are, class is a significant and consistent overt or covert influence on their behavior.

The articulation of specific aspects of women's social class memberships can have a strong impact on their behavior. Women's increased objectivity about their social class interests clarifies how they see themselves with respect to social structures beyond their personal milieus (Mills, 1967). Women can become more autonomous only when they realize the strength and extent of social class influences in their lives.

Identity empowerment occurs most effectively when the impact of class is delineated realistically and dealt with directly—through discussion, decision-making, and action. Identity empowerment, through women's deliberate selections of specific values as sources of their motivation, frequently results in women having increased class mobility, as well as increased autonomy.

Culture

Culture is made up of the plurality of society's majority and minority values and is frequently polarized between traditional and modern values. Mainstream values generally have a stronger influence on women's behavior than marginal values, even when women are members of minority ethnic groups.

Dominant cultural values are a significant social context through which women can increase their understanding of their personal behavior and value negotiations. Culture can be thought of as an infinite variety of value negotiations, which cumulatively shape shared concerns and public issues. In times of rapid social change—such as recent shifts in gender role expectations and standards of sexual behavior—cultural values become ambiguous, and individual and social action may be disoriented.

Society

Society is the most comprehensive social structure with which an individual identifies. The concept of society assumes specific images of history and evolution and related views of the universe (Teilhard de Chardin, 1965). Society suggests the broadest contexts of being.

A marked degree of correspondence between women's perceptions of the universe and the world as it actually exists empowers their identities and behavior. Identity empowerment rests on women's abilities to articulate their most meaningful and representative views of themselves, the world, and the universe.

A focus on the concept of society serves to expand women's awareness of their possibilities and identities. Placing the self in its broadest possible context increases women's abilities to transcend the restrictive empirical realities of their life situations. Greater self-knowledge and identity empowerment are achieved through applying these broad perspectives to their experiences.

IMPLICATIONS

Identity empowerment theory suggests that women's understanding of the strengths and weaknesses of their personal and collective past and present will increase their sense of purpose and direction for the future. Through examination of their values, women become more able to consciously determine lifetime goals in their own interests.

Identity empowerment increases women's knowledge about their options in everyday life. In time, they become more able to cope with conflict in their relationships, although initially they may be perceived by other people as being less productive or less cooperative than they were previously. Identity empowerment necessarily entails some disruption of the status quo, because it is established relationships that are problematic for most women.

The increased breadth and clarity of women's views of society and the universe can motivate them to articulate new values and goals. When women's attention shifts from their personal troubles to social issues, they can more consciously connect their biographies with the historical times in which they live (Mills, 1967). Moreover, attention to the value components of women's behavior increases their motivation for meaningful individual and social actions (Weber, 1964).

Although identity empowerment theory needs much additional substantiation, patterns in women's behavior are discernible, and tentative predictions can be made from the repeated trends in women's interpersonal and collective behavior. Furthermore, the clinical use of identity empowerment theory suggests that, when women choose to make changes in their lives, they can accomplish sometimes dramatic shifts in their life courses.

Legislative changes must remain women's highest priorities in both traditional and modern patriarchal societies. However, other kinds of changes can transform significantly the quality of women's lives. The advantage of working toward changes in values and levels of functioning is that these are not dependent on legislated equality between women and men. Women can claim their equality and then work toward the legislative equality that needs to be attained. As long as women remain in positions of subjugation, they have much work to do to heighten their awareness and to free themselves.

Ideal Types: Subjugated/ Empowered Women

To illustrate some of the contrasts between women who are subjugated and women who are empowered, two ideal types—or hypothetical profiles—are presented: subjugated women and empowered women. Although most women are neither completely subjugated nor completely empowered, some of the major substantive differences among women's radically diverse experiences can be understood by examining these two particular constellations of women's attitudes, values, and behavior.

The two ideal types are derived from a wide range of data drawn from women in families, religion, and work in different cultural settings. The constructs reflect and represent some of the women whose behavior is examined, but they are a composite of all the data collected. The purpose of presenting these two ideal types is to provide a symbolic communication of some of the most pertinent empirical generalizations about women's behavior, rather than to substantiate a specific hypothesis.

Two contrasting sets of empirical generalizations are substantive sources for the construction of the two ideal types of subjugation and empowerment.

The data are used selectively to highlight the wide diversity found in women's attitudes, values, and behavior.

In reality, most women's activities fall somewhere on the continuum between subjugation and empowerment. However, distinguishing between these two particular, more or less coherent sets of possibilities for women deepens understanding about the different situations and responses of women in contrasting age groups, ethnic groups, social classes, historical periods, and cultures.

SUBJUGATED WOMEN

Because most of the societies existing in the world today are patriarchal societies, it can be hypothesized that most women in the world are in relatively subjugated or subordinate social statuses. The ideal type of subjugated woman represents the life chances, attitudes, values, and behavior of women who have adapted to patriarchal structures in both traditional societies and modern, industrialized societies.

Subjugated women's values are essentially defined by men's values. Subjugated women's values are complementary and adaptive to the male hierarchy, and women's moral standards are based on the rationale of maintaining the status quo of dominant male values.

The behavior of subjugated women flows automatically from their allegiance to values defined by the traditional male hierarchy. Male authority structures—and the power resources of males—control subjugated women, with the result that women's life chances are specified only in relation to these patriarchal structures. When subjugated women adhere to values or behavior that are not accepted by the male-dominated standards of their society, they are severely morally, emotionally, mentally, or physically sanctioned.

Subjugated women find it very difficult—if not impossible—to change their functioning positions in traditional male hierarchies. Whether they act in the context of their families, religion, or work, subjugated women are expected to maintain their subordinate roles and to stay within those expectations.

Male-dominated social pressures limit the life chances of subjugated women. Their choices are essentially predetermined, if they are to gain social approval for their behavior.

Subjugated women live most of their lives in very restricted personal milieus, extending themselves very little beyond their traditional family domains. Their visions are limited to the confines of their interpersonal networks, and their goals cannot go beyond maintaining family relationships and the wellbeing of family members.

Subjugated women's responsibilities are endorsed by their religious beliefs. Their private worlds are far removed from the public worlds of men, and their work generally consists of doing unpaid domestic chores or agricultural labor in the home setting.

EMPOWERED WOMEN

Empowered women define their attitudes, values, and behavior in relation to their own real interests. They have autonomy because they claim their freedom from existing male hierarchies, whether they live in traditional societies or modern, industrial societies.

Empowered women maintain equal-mindedness, rather than act out roles that merely confront and challenge male dominance. Empowered women do not aim at being superior to men. They respond as equals and cooperate in order to work toward the common good.

Empowered women use their talents to live fulfilling lives. They have not only survived the harshness of their own subjugation, but they have also transcended their subjugation, thus moving themselves through survival to fulfillment. Empowered women maintain their strength in the presence of pressures of family, religion, and work, and they contribute toward the empowerment of all women.

Empowered women are aware of their own uniqueness and, at the same time, of their collective belonging with other women. They know that their individual good and welfare can only be viewed and understood with reference to the well-being of all women. They cannot be empowered at the expense of other women or of men.

Empowered women may continue to meet their family responsibilities and participate in religion. They choose to do so in ways that strengthen rather than debilitate them, however, which is also advantageous for others. Empowered women do not retreat from these traditional responsibilities, but rather forge their own ways of doing things.

Empowered women define their values and formulate their beliefs themselves. They do not derive their sense of being from male authorities, and they do not live vicariously through men. Empowered women strengthen themselves through other women's support and sustain their own moral visions. Their actions flow from their own distinctive ideals.

Empowered women can be found in all social groups and all societies. However, the optimal conditions for empowered women are both individual and social, and there are more empowered women in modern societies, because the collective actions of women are more visible and more palpable in those settings.

Glossary

The following terms are central to descriptions and discussions in *Women and Empowerment*, and where appropriate, special meanings and connotations in relation to women and empowerment are stated briefly.

Activism   Behavior directed toward specific social changes; participation in an organized (or unorganized) social movement.

Age   Category of social stratification; meaningful unit of analysis in examining social behavior; chronological cohort.

Analysis   Examination of given facts to determine a scientific or objective explanation.

Attitude   Emotional and value orientation to self, others, and the world.

Authority structure   Hierarchy of male values that is the essence of patriarchy.

Automatic behavior   Conditioned response or reaction; behavior that is not reflective or deliberate.

Autonomy   Ability to make one's own decisions and take action accordingly, regardless of pressure brought by others; meaningful management of one's own time and energy.

Awareness   Consciousness or knowledge of self and the world; attention paid to the facts of existence.

Belief system   Internalized views of reality; established priorities and preferences that may be integrated with religion or myth.

Biography   Facts and impressions about life-time experience; listing of significant events or turning points that have changed the quality of one's life.

Career   Education and development of talents in a direction of related work opportunities; long-range creation of professional or artistic skills.

Choice   Critical selection of behavioral outcomes; awareness of and decisions about options in different situations.

Classical sociological theory   Founding theories of the discipline of sociology, developed in nineteenth and early twentieth centuries; includes broad theories of society concerned with social reconstruction after French and Industrial revolutions.

Clinical sociology   Subdivision of applied sociology or sociological practice; level of analysis that places an individual in family, small group, and community contexts; discipline that focuses on crisis intervention and the application of sociological theory to achieve constructive change.

Community   Large local network of at least several hundred individuals; includes special interest or occupational groups.

Concept   Idea that can be operationalized for scientific research; unit or building block of theory.

Conditioning   Internalization of social controls that restrict how behavioral options are experienced; social influences that precipitate automatic, limited reactions.

Contemporary sociological theory   Recent theoretical developments in discipline of sociology; includes world system, comparative development, and middle-range theories with limited substantive scope.

Crisis intervention   Deliberate action or application of strategies to change behavior and relationship patterns of people in crises.

Culture   Meaningful context of behavior; accumulated values and moral standards of society; characteristic constellations of norms can be distinguished as traditional or modern cultures.

Definition of the situation   Articulated view and understanding of facts about an immediate reality; beliefs about present circumstances that strongly influence decisionmaking and behavior.

Denomination   Major, mainstream organization within a world religion.

Division of labor   Specialization of work/tasks to meet society's needs for survival and achievement; economic organization that has rationale of efficiency and tradition of accomplishment; economic base of social stratification.

Documentation   Formal verification, substantiation, or refutation of specific hypotheses or propositions; assembly or selection of facts to illustrate, support, or endorse theoretical generalizations.

Dominance   Forceful subordination of individuals who have less power; control of other people's values, choices, and behavior.

Dual-earner family   Family with both spouses working outside of the home; occupations may not be characterized as "professional," especially in the case of positions held by women; presently the predominant nuclear family form in the United States and other highly industrialized countries.

Dyad   An intrinsically unstable two-person relationship; pattern of dominance may exist, although norm of reciprocity brings some balance and continuity to dyadic exchanges.

Emotional system   Intense, interdependent, reactive relationships; the nuclear family is a prototype of an emotional system; work systems and other groups also may be viewed as emotional systems.

Empirical data   Facts and information that can be measured or numerically rated in order to mathematically or qualitatively estimate the impact of specific influences on behavior.

Empowerment   Individual and collective strengthening of negotiating position in relation to the negotiating position of other people; development, growth, and maturation of real talents and aptitudes; recognition and responsibility as an equal.

Equality   Ideal of equal worth; right to have equal opportunities in all spheres of social life.

Equity   Just distribution of economic and social resources; equal access to resources.

Ethnic group   Ascribed, hereditary membership based on race nor achieved membership based on cultural distinctiveness; religious affiliation is included in complex of shared characteristics.

Evolution   Broadest possible trends in growth, change, and development of animal, vegetable, and mineral forms; complex mutations and processes that are measured in geological time units.

Expectations   Individual and social norms and standards based on a significant degree of consensus; social controls that limit behavioral options.

Facts   External events and occurrences that can be measured; information about circumstances that is gathered to give meaning to those circumstances.

Family   Most basic human group that meets fundamental survival needs of individuals and society; life-time membership of the family is based on kinship, contract, or adoption; source of most intense human and social conditioning in early developmental stages.

Feminism   Organized political ideology that underpins women's social movement to achieve ideal of equality between women and men.

Focus   Emphasis; center of interest; substance of central hypothesis.

Freedom   Ability to act autonomously from the base of one's own values and interests; social conditions that promote equal opportunities for all.

Friendship   Informal mutual support between two or more parties; relationships with more or less equal participation and reciprocity; a voluntary association with another person that may be terminated at any time, but that may also last a life time.

Fulfillment   Satisfaction that derives from aligning individual interests with contributions to social needs.

Functioning   Constructive behavior and action; behavior that matches capacity and potential in some crucial respects.

Gender   Female or male essence of self; conditioned, learned behavior that meets social expectations associated with being female or male.

Generalization   Statement about common experiences or shared trends; association of observations or overview of research findings about particular aspects of behavior.

Goal   Objective or desired result that can be achieved; end product that may motivate behavior.

Grassroots   Individual level of political activism or expression of rights; source and substance of collective social action.

Growth   Personal change in attitudes and behavior, in the direction of maturation and empowerment.

Health   Balance in physical, mental, emotional, spiritual, and social functioning.

Hierarchy   Vertical organization of individuals or groups with unequal power or resources.

History   National and international changes that have been described (and taken for granted) in terms of mainstream political interests; politically significant trends and events that are organized according to chronologies of decades or centuries.

Honesty   Attempt to see through romance, denial, and hypocrisy; objective view of self, others, and situations; critical examination of facts and perceptions.

Human nature   Raw essence of being and behavior; given biological tendencies, together with basic learned behavior at survival level.

Human rights   Equality for all; protection of fundamental needs.

Hypothetical   Tentative, reasoned speculation about the nature of reality; the formulation of a theoretical proposition for empirical substantiation or refutation.

Ideal   Perfect, utopian state to which one aspires; social prescription that transcends reality; powerful source of motivation when stated as objective to be accomplished.

Ideal type   Hypothetical construct that represents an individual or social phenomenon; characteristic profile of personal or collective human behavior, which is systematically abstracted from actual data on that behavior.

Identity   Basic values that one considers to be one's own; orientation of self to others and the world at large; a felt connection with specific activities or groups.

Identity empowerment theory   Description and explanation of how people align self with their most significant values, groups, and activities in society.

Ideology   Political, secular belief system; rationale for collective behavior or social movement promoting specific kinds of change.

Image   Picture or presentation of who we think we would like to be or of who we think we might be.

Independence   Autonomy; economic source of social status; ability to make one's own decisions, control one's own resources, and avail oneself of significant social resources.

Interdependence   Satisfactorily balanced relatedness with other people; ability to express adequate give and take in social negotiations.

Interest   Behavior organized around attaining goals that reflect special needs or aspirations; expression of most cherished values.

Interpretation   Meaning derived from examining facts.

Job   Paid activity that accomplishes chores or occupational specifications.

Life history   Overview of events and circumstances of a life time; biography; collection of facts about major changes or turning points experienced in living.

Life-satisfaction   Fulfillment of valued goals; meaningful everyday behavior.

Macrosociology   Broadest substantive theories about society, social change, and social institutions.

Maturity   Personal growth; empowerment; functional move toward independence.

Meaningful contact   Quality one-on-one relationship, based on equal worth and equal-mindedness.

Methodology   System of study; steps in applying a theory or concept; specification of means designed to substantiate or refute a particular hypothesis.

Microsociology   Sociological analysis of small groups, families, and interpersonal interaction.

Milieu   Immediate social environment or circumstances; small group context; domestic setting.

Motivation   Social sources of orientation and behavior; ideals and values that induce action.

Mutual support   Social connections that are indubitably constructive and resourceful; function of self-help or self-realization group.

Myth   Fictional narrative or rationale that supports a romantic or unreal view of self, others, and the world; distortion of truth that may be held to be true.

Objectivity   Commitment to maintain a posture that views reality as it is; effort to deliberately neutralize one's biases and vested interest.

Oppression   Coerced subordination of the powerless by the powerful.

Optimal conditions   Social structures and influences that support the most constructive behavioral outcomes.

Orientation   World view; most deep-seated attitudes toward others.

Paradigm   Basic theoretical axioms that form the essence of a particular definition of reality.

Patriarchy   Male-dominated social hierarchy in society; male-dominated authority structure that permeates all social relations; institutionalized male dominance.

Pattern of behavior   Repeated regularities in interpersonal behavior; predictable reactions in group exchanges.

Pawn   Individual living by automatic, determined behavior resulting from social conditioning; passive victim of circumstances.

Possibility   Option that exists, but may not be acknowledged or chosen.

Predictability   Scientific forecast of behavior or trends that are likely to happen; determination of conditions that lead to the occurrence of an event or manifestation of a phenomenon.

Pressure   Power of other people's expectations; controls that restrict behavior.

Priority   Preferred goal, behavior, or values.

Probability   Degree of likelihood that an individual or group will behave in specified ways.

Proposition   Tentative hypothesis about a correlation of variables.

Public life   Behavior in community or social setting; domain that has been monopolized historically by males in traditional societies and to a large extent in modern industrial societies.

Reference group   Significant association with others, through actual membership or desired membership; meaningful source of identity with people with shared interests.

Relationship   Continued sequence of intimate interaction with one other person or a few other people.

Religion   Beliefs and practices related to a supernatural being or a divine order; denominational and sectarian traditions based on the assumption of a sacred or moral universe.

Remuneration   Financial compensation for work accomplished.

Research   Systematic study; application of objective methodology in order to make a substantive contribution to science or other forms of knowledge.

Responsibility   Deliberate ownership of one's own thoughts, feelings, and actions; acting with awareness and consideration for the consequences of one's behavior.

Role   Behavioral prescription for a particular status; the performance of expected acts and duties.

Sanction   Verbal, mental, physical, or spiritual reprimand or punishment for aberrant or deviant behavior.

Science   Objective knowledge based on laws of the natural order of the universe.

Sect   Small religious group that does not conform to the beliefs or practices of larger, more established denominations.

Self   Personal core or center of an individual's deepest source of identity; synthesis or distillation of one's nonnegotiable values and convictions.

Sex   Biological, hereditary attribute of male or female genes.

Significant others   Those who are emotionally closest to one; one's most meaningful relationships.

Social class   Social group or category defined by criteria such as sex, age, economic means, and ethnic characteristics.

Social control   External restraint through sanctions, together with internalized inhibition or restriction on behavior.

Socialization   Developmental process characterized by the influence of external controls and the internalization of values.

Social structure   Institutionalized regularities in patterns of interaction; established procedures for meeting basic social needs; codified and/or inflexibly incorporated social influences and practices.

Society   Nation-state; broadest legal and political context of social behavior and social organization.

Sociological practice   Applied sociology; sociological analysis of policy and program evaluation; application of sociological theory in crisis intervention.

Spirituality   Emphasis on spirit as the essence of humanity; mystical development; personal transcendence of empirical realities.

Standards   Objective norms or criteria that are accepted or acknowledged by a majority of people as having representative value; may be believed to be legitimate and true.

Status   Social standing directly related to roles played in the community, education, occupation, and economy.

Stereotype   Distorted understanding of behavior that is mistakenly considered to be representative of a particular group or an average; faulty perception that becomes a source of prejudice and discrimination; alien objectification of personal or group characteristics.

Strategy   Planned line of action directed at accomplishing a specific objective; clinical technique or political ploy.

Subjectivity   Individual perception of reality that may be eccentric, idiosyncratic, and not shared by other people; view of the world that is personal rather than objective.

Subjugation   Oppression of less powerful people by those with more power; condition of being restricted or coerced by authorities.

Subordination   Acceptance of unequal standing; shared placement in a less advantageous social position.

Substantiation   Collection and organization of data to prove a hypothesis or demonstrate truth.

Survival   Adaptation; staying alive and functioning adequately in face of the possibility of extinction.

Theory   Series of interrelated, integrated propositions that accurately represent reality.

Tradition   Established sets of procedures and practices that have been tested through long periods of time and handed down by successive generations.

Triad   Three-person relationship system; most stable unit of a group or large social organization.

Understanding   Knowing at a deep emotional level what a situation really is or who someone really is.

Value   Desired objective of individuals and groups; shared, cherished ideal or practice; established or recognized benefit.

Violence   Physical, emotional, mental, or social abuse through the manipulation of power, coercion, or persuasion; victimization.

Vision   Utopian ideal or dream of perfection that transcends an actual situation; perception of possibilities in spite of difficult or hopeless circumstances.

Welfare state   Country with legislation and programs that protect and support citizens with special needs; governmental provision of direct services to improve the quality of life for all.

Well-being   Advantageous condition of satisfaction and meaningful fulfillment.

Women's studies   Interdisciplinary scholarship about women and women's concerns; knowledge derived and developed relatively recently from women's perceptions and experiences.

Work   Paid and unpaid labor, performed in or out of the home, that may or may not be related to career development; includes domestic or agricultural chores, jobs not characterized as professions or professionally oriented, as well as intense effort in one occupation.

World view   Orientation of values and beliefs toward the universe; perception of contrasting cultures and different historical periods.

Bibliography

Aga, S. (1984). I'll never go back to women's work again! *Women's Studies International Forum, 7,* 441–448.

Aldous, J. (Ed.). (1982). *Two paychecks: Life in dual-earner families.* Beverly Hills: Sage.

Alland, A. (1967). *Evolution and Human Behavior.* Garden City, NY: Natural History Press.

Andersen, M. L. (1988). *Thinking about women: Sociological and feminist perspectives.* 2nd ed. New York: Macmillan.

Aries, P. (1965). *Centuries of childhood.* New York: Random House.

Aytac, I. (1990). Sharing household tasks in the United States and Sweden: A reassessment of Kohn's theory. *Sociological Spectrum, 10,* 357–371.

Baxter, S., & Lansing, M. (1983). *Women and politics: The visible majority.* Ann Arbor: University of Michigan Press.

Beard, M. (1971). *Woman as force in history.* New York: Collier.

Beauvoir, S. de. (1974). *The second sex.* New York: Random House. (Original work published 1949.)

Becker, H. S. (1950). *Through values to social interpretation.* Durham, NC: Duke University Press.

Bell, R. R. (1981). *Worlds of friendship*. Beverly Hills: Sage.

Berger, B. M. (Ed.). (1990). *Authors of their own lives: Intellectual autobiographies by twenty American sociologists*. Berkeley: University of California Press.

Berger, P. L., & Luckmann, T. (1966). *The social construction of reality*. Garden City, NY: Doubleday.

Bergmann, B. (1981). The economic risks of being a housewife. *American Economic Review, 71*, 81–86.

Bernard, J. (1971). *Women and the public interest*. Chicago: Aldine.

Bernard, J. (1981). *The female world*. New York: Free Press.

Berteaux, D. (1981). *Biography and society: The life history approach in the social sciences*. Beverly Hills: Sage.

Blau, P. M. (1967). *Exchange and power in social life*. New York: Wiley.

Blumer, H. (1969). *Symbolic interaction: Perspective and method*. Englewood Cliffs, NJ: Prentice-Hall.

Bose, C., Feldbera, R., & Sokoloff, N. (Eds.). (1987). *Hidden aspects of women's work*. New York: Praeger.

Bott, E. (1957). *Family and social network: Roles, norms and external relationships in ordinary urban families*. London: Tavistock Publications.

Bowen, M. (1978). *Family therapy in clinical practice*. New York: Aronson.

Bradley, H. (1989). *Men's work, women's work: A sociological history of the sexual division of labor in employment*. Minneapolis: University of Minnesota Press.

Brownmiller, S. (1975). *Against our will: Men, women and rape*. New York: Simon and Schuster.

Burdick, J. (1990). Gossip and secrecy: Women's articulation of domestic conflict in three religions of urban Brazil. *Sociological Analysis, 51*, 153–170.

Cancian, F. M. (1987). *Love in America: Gender and self-development*. New York: Cambridge University Press.

Caplow, T. (1968). *Two against one: Coalitions in triads*. Englewood Cliffs, NJ: Prentice Hall.

Carden, M. L. (1974). *The new feminist movement*. New York: Russell Sage Foundation.

Caute, D. (Ed.). (1967). *Essential writings of Karl Marx*. New York: Collier.

Chafetz, J. S. (1990). *Gender equity: An integrated theory of stability and change*. Newbury Park, CA: Sage.

Chafetz, J. S., & Dworkin, A. (1986). *Female revolt: Women's movements in world and historical perspective*. Totowa, NJ: Rowman and Allanheld.

Charles, N. (1990). Women and class: A problematic relationship? *The Sociological Review, 38*, 43–89.

Charlton, S. E. M., Everett, J., & Staudt, K. (Eds.). (1989). *Women, the state, and development*. Albany: State University of New York Press.

Chernin, K. (1981). *The obsession: Reflections on the tyranny of slenderness*. New York: Harper and Row.

Chodorow, N. J. (1978). *The reproduction of mothering: Psychoanalysis and the sociology of gender*. Berkeley: University of California Press.

Chodorow, N. J. (1989). *Feminism and psychoanalytic theory*. New Haven: Yale University Press.

Christ, C. P. (1983). Heretics and outsiders: The struggle over female power in Western religion. In L. Richardson & V. Taylor (Eds.), *Feminist frontiers* (pp. 87–94). Reading, MA: Addison-Wesley.

Christ, C. P., & Plaskow, J. (Eds.). (1979). *Womanspirit rising.* New York: Harper and Row.

Clark, E. J. (1990). The development of contemporary clinical sociology. *Clinical Sociology Review, 8,* 100–115.

Cohn, C. (1989). Sex and death in the rational world of defense intellectuals. In M. R. Malson, J. F. O'Barr, S. W. Wihl, & M. Wyer (Eds.), *Feminist theory in practice and process* (pp. 107–136). Chicago: University of Chicago Press.

Coleman, M. T. (1988). The division of household labor: suggestions for future empirical consideration and theoretical development. *Journal of Family Issues, 9,* 132–183.

Condon, J. (1985). *A half step behind: Japanese women of the '80s.* New York: Dodd, Mead.

Cooley, C. H. (1962). *Social organization: A study of the larger mind.* New York: Schocken. (Original work published 1909.)

Cooley, C. H. (1964). *Human nature and the social order.* New York: Schocken. (Original work published 1902.)

Coward, R. (1984). *Female desire: Women's sexuality today.* London: Paladin.

Curtis, R. F. (1986). Household and family in theory on inequality. *American Sociological Review, 51,* 168–183.

Curtis, R. F., & MacCorquodale, P. (1990). Stability and change in gender relations. *Sociological Theory, 8,* 136–152.

Dahrendorf, R. (1959). *Class and class conflict in industrial society.* Stanford: Stanford University Press.

Daly, M. (1968). *The church and the second sex.* New York: Harper and Row.

Daly, M. (1973). *Beyond God the Father: Towards a philosophy of women's liberation.* Boston: Beacon Press.

Davies, K., & Esseveld, J. (1982). Unemployment and identity: A study of women outside the labor market. *Acta Sociologica, 25,* 283–293.

Davis, A. Y. (1983). *Women, race and class.* New York: Vintage.

Dencik, L. (1989). Growing up in the Post-Modern Age: On the child's situation in the modern family, and on the position of the family in the modern welfare state. *Acta Sociologica, 25,* 283–293.

Della Fave, L. R. (1980). The meek shall not inherit the earth: self-evaluation and the legitimacy of stratification. *American Sociological Review, 45,* 955–971.

Diaz-Diocaretz, M., & Zavala, I. M. (Eds.). (1985). *Women, feminist identity and society in the 1980's: Selected papers.* Philadelphia: John Benjamins Publishing Company.

Dinnerstein, D. (1976). *The mermaid and the minotaur: Sexual arrangements and human malaise.* New York: Harper and Row.

Dowling, C. (1982). *The Cinderella complex: Women's hidden fear of independence.* New York: Pocket Books.

Duchen, C. (Ed. & Trans.). (1987). *French connections: Voices from the women's movement in France.* Amherst: The University of Massachusetts Press.

Durkheim, E. (1965). *The elementary forms of the religious life.* New York: Free Press. (Original work published 1912.)

Durkheim, E. (1966). *Suicide.* New York: Free Press. (Original work published 1897.)

Durkheim, E. (1984). *The division of labor in society.* New York: Free Press. (Original work published 1893.)

Eisenstein, Z. (Ed.). (1979). *Capitalist patriarchy and the case for socialist feminism.* New York: Monthly Review Press.

Engels, F. (1970). *The origin of the family, private property and the state.* New York: International Publishers. (Original work published 1884.)

Epstein, C. F., & Coser, R. L. (Eds.). (1981). *Access to power: Cross-national studies of women and elites.* Boston: Allen and Unwin.

Estep, R. E., Burt, M. R., & Milligan, H. J. (1977). The socialization of sexual identity. *Journal of Marriage and the Family, 39,* 99–112.

Evans, R. J. (1977). *The feminists: Women's emancipation movements in Europe, America, and Australia, 1840–1920.* New York: Barnes and Noble.

Feinstein, K. F. (Ed.). (1979). *Working women and families.* Beverly Hills: Sage.

Finkelhor, D., & Gelles, R. J. (Eds.). (1983). *The dark side of families: Current family violence research.* Beverly Hills: Sage.

Firestone, S. (1971). *The dialectic of sex: The case for a feminist revolution.* London: Paladin.

Fitzpatrick, E. (1990). *Endless crusade: Women social scientists and progressive reform.* New York: Oxford University Press.

Flanz, G. H. (1983). *Comparative women's rights and political participation in Europe.* Ardsley-on-Hudson, NY: Transnational Publishers.

Flowers, R. B. (1987). *Women and criminality: The woman as victim, offender, and practitioner.* Westport, CT: Greenwood Press.

Foner, A., & Kertzer, D. (1978). Transition over the life course: lessons from age-set societies. *American Journal of Sociology, 83,* 1081–1104.

Franks, D. D., & McCarthy, E. D. (Eds.). (1989). *The sociology of emotions: Original essays and research papers.* Greenwich, CT: JAI Press.

Frazier, E. F. (1939). *The Negro family in the United States.* Chicago: University of Chicago Press.

Freud, S. (1982). *Three essays on the theory of sexuality.* New York: Basic Books.

Friday, N. (1977). *My mother, my self.* New York: Dell.

Friedan, B. (1963). *The feminine mystique.* New York: Dell.

Friedan, B. (1981). *The second stage.* New York: Summit.

Fritz, J. (1985). *The clinical sociology handbook.* New York: Garland.

Garcia de Leon, M. A. (August, 1990). Discriminated elite—Spanish women in politics. Paper presented at XII International Congress of Sociology, Madrid.

Gelles, R. J. (1979). *Family violence.* Beverly Hills: Sage.

Gerson, K. (1985). *Hard choices: How women decide about work, career, and motherhood.* Berkeley: University of California Press.

Gerth, H. H., & Mills, C. W. (Eds.). (1946). *From Max Weber.* New York: Oxford University Press.

Gilligan, C. (1982). *In a different voice: Psychological theory and women's development.* Cambridge, MA: Harvard University Press.

Glass, J. (1979). Renewing an old profession: Clinical sociology. *American Behavioral Scientist, 22,* 513–529.

Glass, J., & Fritz, J. (1982). Clinical sociology: Origins and development. *Clinical Sociology Review, 1,* 3–6.

Glassner, B., & Freedman, J. A. (1979). *Clinical sociology.* New York: Longman.

Glick, P. C. (1985). Black families. In J. M. Henslin (Ed.), *Marriage and family in a changing society* (pp. 120–132). New York: Macmillan.

Goffman, E. (1973). *The presentation of self in everyday life.* New York: Overlook Press. (Original work published 1959.)

Goode, W. J. (1963). *World revolution and family patterns.* New York: Free Press.

Gordon, M. M. (1988). *The scope of sociology.* New York: Oxford University Press.

Greer, G. (1971). *The female eunuch.* New York: McGraw-Hill.

Gutek, B. (1985). *Sex and the workplace.* San Francisco: Jossey Bass.

Haas, L. (1981). Domestic role sharing in Sweden. *Journal of Marriage and the Family, 43,* 957–963.

Haddad, Y. Y., & Findly, E. B. (Eds.). (1985). *Women, religion, and social change.* Albany: State University of New York Press.

Hall, C. M. (1979). *Woman unliberated: Difficulties and limitations in changing self.* New York: Hemisphere.

Hall, C. M. (1983). *The Bowen family theory and its uses.* New York: Aronson.

Hall, C. M. (1989). Triadic analysis: A conceptual tool for clinical sociologists. *Clinical Sociology Review, 7,* 97–110.

Hall, C. M. (1990a). *Women and identity—value choices in a changing world.* New York: Hemisphere.

Hall, C. M. (1990b). Identity empowerment through clinical sociology. *Clinical Sociology Review, 8,* 69–86.

Hall, C. M. (1991). Clinical sociology and religion. *Clinical Sociology Review, 9,* 48–58.

Hammond, P. E. (1988). Religion and the persistence of identity. *Journal for the Scientific Study of Religion, 27,* 1–11.

Hays, H. R. (1964). *The dangerous sex.* New York: Putnam.

Heckscher, G. (1984). *The welfare state and beyond: Success and problems in Scandinavia.* Minneapolis: University of Minnesota Press.

Hess, B. B., Markson, E. W., & Stein, P. J. (1988). *Sociology* (3rd ed.). New York: Macmillan.

Hewitt, J. P. (1990). *Dilemmas of the American self.* Philadelphia: Temple University Press.

Hill, R. B. (1972). *The strengths of Black families.* New York: Emerson Hall.

Hiller, D. V., & Philliber, W. W. (1986). The division of labor in contemporary marriage: expectations, perceptions and performance. *Social Problems, 33,* 191–201.

Hindberg, B. O. (1988). Violence against women. *Women and Health, 13,* 151–158.

Holter, H. (Ed.). (1984). *Patriarchy in a welfare society.* New York: Columbia University Press.

Homans, G. (1961). *Social behavior: Its elementary forms.* New York: Harcourt, Brace, and World.

Hood, J. C. (1983). *Becoming a two-job family.* New York: Praeger.

Horner, M. (1972). Toward an understanding of achievement related conflicts in women. *Journal of Social Issues, 28,* 157-175.

Howe, L. K. (1977). *Pink collar workers: Inside the world of women's work.* New York: Avon.

Iglitzin, L., & Ross, R. (Eds.). (1986). *Women in the world, 1975-1985: The women's decade.* Oxford, England: Clio Press.

Intons-Peterson, M. J. (1988). *Gender concepts of Swedish and American youth.* Hillsdale, NJ: Lawrence Erlbaum Associates.

Kahn-Hut, R., Daniels, A. K., & Colvard, R. (Eds.). (1982). *Women and work: Problems and perspectives.* New York: Oxford University Press.

Kandal, T. R. (1988). *The woman question in classical sociological theory.* Miami: Florida International University Press.

Kanter, R. M. (1977). *Men and women of the corporation.* New York: Basic Books.

Kauppinen, K., Haavio-Mannila, E., & Kandolin, I. (1989). Who benefits from working in non-traditional workroles: Interaction patterns and quality of worklife. *Acta Sociologica, 32,* 389-403.

Kerr, M., & Bowen, M. (1988). *Family evaluation—an approach based on Bowen theory.* New York: W.W. Norton.

Kessler-Harris, A. (1981). *Women have always worked: A historical overview.* New York: McGraw-Hill.

Kessler-Harris, A. (1982). *Out of work: A history of wage-earning women in the United States.* New York: Oxford University Press.

Kluckhohn, F. R., & Strodtbeck, F. L. (1961). *Variations in value orientations.* Evanston, IL: Row, Peterson.

Kuhn, T. (1970). *The structure of scientific revolution.* Chicago: University of Chicago Press.

Larsson, B., & Olson, H. (1988). The Gotland house: Family relations through four generations in rural Sweden. *Women and Health, 13,* 133-150.

Lee, A. M. (1979). The services of clinical sociology. *American Behavioral Scientist, 22,* 487-511.

Lengermann, P. M., & Wallace, R. A. (1985). *Gender in America—social control and social change.* Englewood Cliffs, NJ: Prentice-Hall.

Lerner, G. (1986). *The creation of patriarchy.* New York: Oxford University Press.

Levy, M. J. (1989). *Our mother-tempers.* Berkeley: University of California Press.

Lindsay, B. (Ed.). (1980). *Perspectives of Third World women.* New York: Praeger.

Linton, R. (1936). *The study of man.* New York: Appleton-Century.

Lipman-Blumen, J. (1984). *Gender roles and power.* Englewood Cliffs, NJ: Prentice-Hall.

Luckmann, T. (1967). *The invisible religion.* New York: Macmillan.

Malson, M. R., O'Barr, J. F., Wihl, S. W., & Wyer, M. (Eds.). (1989). *Feminist theory in practice and process.* Chicago: University of Chicago Press.

Mander, A. V., & Rush, A. K. (1974). *Feminism as therapy.* New York: Random House.

Mannheim, K. (1936). *Ideology and utopia: An introduction to the sociology of knowledge.* New York: Harcourt, Brace, and World. (Original work published 1929.)

Marks, S. R. (1977). Multiple roles and role strain: some notes on human energy, time and commitment. *American Sociological Review, 42,* 921–936.

Martyna, W. (1980). Beyond the "he/man" approach: The case for nonsexist language. *Signs, 5,* 482–493.

Mason, K. O., & Bumpass, L. (1975). U.S. women's sex-role ideology. *American Journal of Sociology, 80,* 1212–1219.

Mason, K. O., Czajka, J., & Arber, S. (1976). Change in U.S. women's sex-role attitudes, 1964–1974. *American Sociological Review, 41,* 573–596.

Matthaei, J. (1982). *An economic history of women in America.* New York: Schocken.

McCall, G. J., & Simmons, J. L. (1978). *Identities and interactions: An examination of human associations in everyday life.* New York: Free Press.

McKinney, K., & Sprecher, S. (Eds.). (1989). *Human sexuality: The societal and interpersonal context.* Norwood, NJ: Ablex.

Mead, G. H. (1967). *Mind, self, and society.* Chicago: University of Chicago Press. (Original work published 1934.)

Merton, R. K., & Kitt, A. S. (1969). Reference groups. In L. A. Coser & B. Rosenberg (Eds.), *Sociological Theory* (pp. 243–250). New York: Macmillan.

Millett, K. (1970). *Sexual politics.* Garden City, NY: Doubleday.

Mills, C. W. (1967). *The sociological imagination.* New York: Oxford University Press. (Original work published 1959.)

Mitchell, J. (1975). *Psychoanalysis and feminism.* New York: Random House.

Moreno, J. D., & Glassner, B. (1979). Clinical sociology: A social ontology for therapy. *American Behavioral Scientist, 22,* 531–541.

Morgan, R. (1982). *The anatomy of freedom: Feminism, physics and global politics.* Garden City, NY: Anchor.

Oakley, A. (1975). *The sociology of housework.* New York: Pantheon.

Oakley, A. (1976). *Women's work: The housewife, past and present.* New York: Random House.

Oliker, S. J. (1989). *Best friends and marriage: Exchange among women.* Berkeley: University of California Press.

Ozawa, M. N. (Ed.). (1989). *Women's life cycle and economic insecurity: Problems and proposals.* New York: Greenwood Press.

Pearce, D. (1983). The feminization of ghetto poverty. *Society, 21* (November–December), 70–74.

Pescatello, A. (Ed.). (1973). *Female and male in Latin America.* Pittsburgh: University of Pittsburgh Press.

Peterson, R. R. (1989). *Women, work and divorce.* Albany: State University of New York Press.

Plaskow, J. (1983). The coming of Lilith. In L. Richardson & V. Taylor (Eds.), *Feminist frontiers* (pp. 384–385). Reading, MA: Addison-Wesley.

Pleck, J. H. (1985). *Working wives/working husbands.* Beverly Hills: Sage.

Portocarero, L. (1989). Trends in occupational mobility: The gender gap in Sweden. *Acta Sociologica, 32,* 359–374.

Pruitt, D. G. (1981). *Negotiation behavior.* New York: Academic Press.

Randour, M. L. (1987). *Women's psyche, women's spirit.* New York: Columbia University Press.

Rapoport, R., & Rapoport, R. (1971). *Dual-career families.* Harmondsworth, England: Penguin.

Rapoport, R., & Rapoport, R. (1976). *Dual-career families re-examined: New integration of work and family.* New York: Harper and Row.

Reskin, B. (1988). Bringing the men back in: sex differentiation and the devaluation of women's work. *Gender and Society, 2,* 58–81.

Reskin, B., & Hartman, H. I. (Eds.). (1986). *Women's work, men's work: Sex segregation on the job.* Washington, DC: National Academy Press.

Richardson, L. (1988). *The dynamics of sex and gender—a sociological perspective* (3rd ed.). New York: Harper and Row.

Richardson, L., & Taylor, V. (Eds.). (1983). *Feminist frontiers.* Reading, MA: Addison-Wesley.

Robins-Mowry, D. (1983). *The hidden sun: Women of modern Japan.* Boulder, CO: Westview Press.

Roper, B. S., & Labeff, E. (1977). Sex roles and feminism revisited: An intergenerational attitude comparison. *Journal of Marriage and the Family, 39,* 113–119.

Rosaldo, M. Z., & Lamphere, L. (Eds.). (1974). *Woman, culture and society.* Stanford: Stanford University Press.

Rosen, B. C. (1989). *Women, work and achievement: The endless revolution.* New York: St. Martin's Press.

Rosenberg, M. (1979). *Conceiving the self.* New York: Basic Books.

Rosenberg, M., & Turner, R. H. (Eds.). (1981). *Social psychology.* New York: Basic Books.

Ross, C. E. (1987). The division of labor at home. *Social Forces, 65,* 816–833.

Rowbotham, S. (1974). *Women's consciousness, man's world.* New York: Penguin.

Rowbotham, S. (1989). *The past is before us: Feminism in action since the 1960s.* London: Pandora Press.

Ruth, S. (Ed.). (1980). *Issues in feminism.* Boston: Houghton Mifflin.

Sanday, P. R. (1981). *Female power and male dominance.* Cambridge: Cambridge University Press.

Schaef, A. W. (1985). Women's reality: An emerging female system in a White male society. Minneapolis: Winston Press.

Schur, E. M. (1984). *Labeling women deviant: Gender, stigma and social control.* New York: Random House.

Scott, H. (1982). *Sweden's "right to be human" sex-role equality: The goal and the reality.* Armonk, NY: M.E. Sharpe.

Shehan, C. L., Bock, E. W., & Lee, G. R. (1990). Religious heterogamy, religiosity, and marital happiness: The case of Catholics. *Journal of Marriage and the Family, 52,* 73–79.

Shibutani, T. (1955). Reference groups as perspectives. *American Journal of Sociology, 60,* 562–569.

Sieber, S. D. (1974). Toward a theory of role accumulation. *American Sociological Review, 39,* 467–478.

Smelser, N. J. (1962). *The theory of collective behavior.* New York: Free Press.

Spiro, M. E. (1979). *Gender and culture: Kibbutz women revisited.* Durham, NC: Duke University Press.

Staples, R. (1973). *The Black woman in America.* Chicago: Nelson Hill.

Staples, R. (1985). Changes in black family structure: The conflict between family ideology and structural conditions. *Journal of Marriage and the Family, 47,* 1005–1012.

Steinberg, R., & Haignere, L. (1984). *Separate but equivalent: Equal pay for work of comparable worth.* Washington, DC: Women's Research and Education Institute.

Stetson, D. M. (1987). *Women's rights in France.* Westport, CT: Greenwood Press.

Straus, M., Gelles, R., & Steinmetz, S. (1980). *Behind closed doors: Violence in the American family.* Garden City, NY: Anchor/Doubleday.

Straus, R. A. (Ed.). (1985). *Using sociology: An introduction from the clinical perspective.* New York: General Hall.

Strauss, A. (1978). *Negotiations: Varieties, contexts, processes and social order.* San Francisco: Jossey Bass.

Sydie, R. A. (1987). *Natural women, cultured men: A feminist perspective on sociological theory.* New York: New York University Press.

Teilhard de Chardin, P. (1965). *The phenomenon of man.* New York: Harper and Row.

Thomas, W. I. (1931). The relation of research to the social process. In W. F. G. Swann et al. (Eds.), *Essays on research in the social sciences* (pp. 175–194). Washington: Brookings Institution.

Tiryakian, E. A. (1981). Sexual anomie, social structure, societal change. *Social Forces, 59,* 1025–1053.

Trost, J. E. (1984) Remarriage in Sweden. *Family Relations, 33,* 475–481.

Turner, R. H. (1976). The real self: from institution to impulse. *American Journal of Sociology, 81,* 989–1016.

van den Hoogen, L. (1990). The Romanization of the Brazilian church: Women's participation in a religious association in Prados, Minas Gerais. *Sociological Analysis, 51,* 171–188.

Waerness, K., & Ringen, S. (1987). Women in the welfare state: The case of formal and informal old-age care. In R. Erikson, E. J. Hansen, S. Ringer, & H. Uusitalo (Eds.), *The Scandinavian model: Welfare states and welfare research* (pp. 161–173). Armonk, NY: M.E. Sharpe.

Wallace, R. A. (Ed.). (1989). *Feminism and sociological theory.* Newbury Park, CA: Sage.

Weber, M. (1964). *The sociology of religion.* Boston: Beacon Press. (Original work published 1922.)

Weber, M. (1977). *The Protestant ethic and the spirit of capitalism.* New York: Macmillan. (Original work published 1905.)

Weitzman, L. (1979). *Sex role socialization: A focus on women.* Palo Alto, CA: Mayfield.

Weitzman, L. (1985). *Divorce revolution: The unexpected social and economic consequences for women and children in America.* New York: Free Press.

Westwood, S. (1985). *All day, every day: Factory and family in the making of women's lives.* Chicago: University of Illinois Press.

Wilson, W. J. (1980). *The declining significance of race: Blacks and changing American institutions.* Chicago: University of Chicago Press.

Wirth, L. (1931). Clinical sociology. *American Journal of Sociology, 37,* 49–66.

Wolff, K. H. (Ed. and Trans.). (1950). *The sociology of Georg Simmel.* Glencoe, IL: Free Press.

Wollstonecraft, M. (1982). *A vindication of the rights of women.* New York: Penguin. (Original work published 1792.)

Zaretsky, E. (1976). *Capitalism, the family and personal life.* New York: Harper and Row.

Index